# SCENT OF APPLES

# Scent of Apples

A COLLECTION OF STORIES
BY BIENVENIDO N. SANTOS
Introduction by Leonard Casper

UNIVERSITY OF WASHINGTON PRESS

Seattle and London

Copyright © 1955, 1967 by Bienvenido N. Santos
Introduction and Preface © 1979 by the University of Washington Press
Second printing, 1981
Third printing, 1992
Fourth printing, 1994
Printed in the United States of America

"Immigration Blues" first appeared in the June 1977 issue of *New Letters*. "The
Day the Dancers Came," "The Contender," "Quicker with Arrows," and "Footnote to a Laundry List" first appeared in the Philippines in *The Day the Dancers
Came* (Bookmark Press, 1967). The remaining stories in this volume first appeared in the Philippines in *You Lovely People* (Bookmark Press, 1955).

The original edition of this book was published with the aid of a grant from
Wichita State University.

Library of Congress Cataloging-in-Publication Data
Santos, Bienvenido N.
   Scent of apples.
   1. Filipinos in the United States—Fiction.
I. Title.
PZ4.S2375Sc    1979    [PR9550.9.S22]    823    79–4857
ISBN 0–295–95695–X pbk.

The paper used in this publication meets the minimum requirements of American National Standard for Information Sciences—Permanence of Paper for
Printed Library Materials, ANSI Z39.48–1984. ∞

*To my wife, Beatriz*

# CONTENTS

# INTRODUCTION

*In the fall of 1942, Ben Santos was summoned from his studies at* Columbia University and assigned a basement desk in the Information Division of the Commonwealth Building (now the Philippine Embassy) in Washington. Some of the upstairs officials preferred speaking Spanish and, on the avenues, passing as Latin Americans. Near Santos worked Jose Garcia Villa, mindlessly clipping news items about Bataan and Corregidor while lost in reveries about his first volume of poems, just released: *Have Come, Am Here*. Santos' own sentiments were fixed on his homeland and the immeasurable distances placed by war between it and not only the Philippine government-in-exile which he served, but also anxious *pensionados* like himself with endangered families still in the occupied islands.

His enforced separation from his wife and three young daughters brought him closer to fellow "exiles" whom he later met when the U.S. Office of Education asked him to tour America, lecturing on the worth and stamina of Filipinos as allies. "I loved my countrymen," he wrote, "the so-called Pinoys who were simple and good and trusting once they found you were not a snob." His stories about their anguish and strengths were eventually collected in *You Lovely People* (1955). But he has never really ceased to write about these "hurt men," whose isolation he was to share again in the postwar decades, as resident author on Midwest campuses.

The hard circumstances of prewar Filipino immigrants have been recounted too capably in Carey McWilliams' preface to

Carlos Bulosan's *America Is in the Heart* to require repetition. For years, one of the most unnatural conditions imposed on the *sakadas* who cut Hawaiian sugar cane, or the truck-farm *cargadores* of the Imperial Valley, or the transient menials in the rundown neighborhoods of Chicago and New York, was the near absence of Filipino women among them. When women did occasionally appear, they had to defend themselves against attention turned desperate; and their caution, reinforcing Filipino decorum, was often misunderstood. In "Brown Coterie," one of the original collection's nineteen episodes, a number of educated "Filipina girls" are scolded for avoiding the "good-for-nothing boys who circulate around here." In their enforced loneliness, some Filipinos earned a reputation as "blonde chasers"; others sought in American women the virtues of fidelity and tenderness which they associated with the half-remembered, half-romanticized motherland. Novelist-critic N. V. M. Gonzalez is surely correct in seeing this ideal as providing *You Lovely People* with "a heroine, the Filipino woman. Obviously, she is what no woman in the flesh can ever be; still, the hurt men are as if possessed. I suspect that it is their private vision of her which made them different, handsome in their awkward way, and which guaranteed survival of some kind."

Filipinos, like their agrarian counterparts elsewhere, traditionally have enjoyed a highly developed sense of community (*bayanihan*), dependent on face-to-face (*damay*) relations. They have drawn their identity from extended family lines, fortified by very real and multiple ritual godparenthood (*compadrinazco*), even when nearly four hundred years of Spanish overrule and half a century of American sovereignty prevented development of any clear image of national identity. Some of the psychological security derived from supportive family closeness had to be sacrificed by persons migrating to metropolitan Manila or to American fields and canneries, despite the fact that their earnings were shared with those left behind. The Pinoy's isolation became an extension of the pain of separation that other Filipinos felt when transported from one island (and vernacular) to another, or from rural barrios to makeshift *barong-barongs* dangerously propped on the edge of city railroad tracks or slowly collapsing into storm-sewer *esteros*. Furthermore, the feeling of uneasy identity, natural to the Commonwealth years of experiments in political independence, was multiplied among overseas Filipinos because of both physical distances between themselves and their motherland, and the psychological distances between the Pinoys and earlier migrants from Europe and East Asia. In addition to the usual difficulty that all humans have, of negotiating a single selfhood out of *being* and *becoming*, the Pinoy's expectation of *belonging* to others and not just to himself somehow had to be satisfied.

The wonder is that, under all this cultural stress epitomized by the war years' abrupt rupture of family communications, so many Pinoys managed to remain "lovely people." Like Bulosan, Santos can chronicle the varieties of pathetic frustration; the sense of abandonment associated with liberation from a colonial past; the wearing away of protective naivete. But, again like Bulosan, he captures the infallible faith, the resilience, the resurgent dream of self-recognition and esteem, the folk endurance of a people partially immunized against despair by so long a history of dispossession.

The difficulty of reconciling the Filipino dream of solidarity with the American dream of individualism, of unity risking and enriched by diversity, is implied in the mestizo form of *You Lovely People*. Many of its episodes are self-contained; others, with Ben at the circumference or Ambo (Pablo) at their center, provide a kind of continuity compatible with change. Ambo's trembling hands and poker face mirror the Pinoy's profound disquiet under a mask of serenity. Similarly, Ben's near-anonymity barely conceals the fact that whatever is missing in him has to be found in these others, their gentleness, their thoughtless betrayals, their confusions and confessions. Santos deliberately keeps center and circumference subservient to the circle of Pinoy compatriots—such is the book's socioesthetic. Both Ambo and Ben exist in that purest of compassions: shared suffering, as concelebrated offering.

In all of Santos' fiction, this compulsion to belong consistently raised images of departure and provisional return, of loss and attempted recovery. The structure of his second collection of stories, *Brother, My Brother* (1960), is generally recollective of an original flight from the Sulucan slums of Manila to the greater opportunities in the less crowded prewar barrios of Albay under the shadow of Mt. Mayon. Guilt that the relative ease has not been deserved or adequately shared creates an alternating current of tensions not unlike the expatriation/repatriation/reëxpatriation pattern in *You Lovely People*. The same longing for home and homogeneity serves as a central motif for his first novel, *Villa Magdalena* (1965), in which, driven by the smell of death in their tanneries, various members flee the decaying Conde-Medallada ancestral home, for Japan and America. Only years later do they recognize that mortality cannot be outrun, though mutual solicitude may offset it; and a family feeling is restored. A second novel, *The Volcano*, also published in 1965, dramatizes the Filipino crisis of identity by chronicling the lives of an American missionary family in the islands, between 1928 and 1958. Cross-cultural relationships at first rise smoothly; then, as a Philippine-American marriage is planned, abruptly drop. The sharp contours of the action resemble the perfect cone of Mt. Mayon, beneath whose picturesque slopes seethes a molten mass in perpetual threat of eruption. When ultranationalists violently demand that the Americans return to a country they have hardly known, for the first time they too experience (without quite appreciating) the Filipino's long-term sense of deprivation and homelessness.

In the May 1971–February 1972 issues of *Solidarity*, a Manila monthly, Santos serialized *The Praying Man*, a novel about a slum-dweller from Sulucan who becomes a multimillionaire by selling diluted drugs with the aid of government functionaries. (His wife remarks, "He has to meet, you know, the high cost of bribing.") But even though Santos implies that group-loyalty precious to Filipinos can so corrupt their feeling of community that it deteriorates into special-interest complicities, still he affirms its more positive side. What comforts the fugitive from justice is not the prospect of spending funds salted away in Swiss banks, but the trustworthiness he discovers in two persons from Sulucan, especially his best friend who is now a sculptor in Chicago. Penitent and unafraid, he returns from the States to face charges. The sculptor too is restored by that bond of friendship. He has been laboring on a cryptic memorial to a Sulucan eyesore, a man who daily lay naked and withered, "like the praying mantis," on a pallet near an open window: fatally diseased, yet refusing to die. Out of spite? Out of fear? By the end of the novel, the sculptor has recast his bronze in an attitude of courageous hope. Neither the millionaire's countless *queridas* nor the sculptor's affair of confused passion with Mabel, a student at Northwestern, has offered adequate "pain-killers for loneliness." However, the two men's friendship succeeds because it springs from Sulucan—symbol, in Santos, for folk loyalty and support; help from the helpless, in the absence of patrons.

The feeling of being a displaced person—of having lost or betrayed the traditional attitudes that ordered society—is inevitable in any society undergoing relatively rapid change. The reaction can be as violent as the revolutionary fervor which characterized the Sakdalista movement during the Commonwealth years, the postwar Huk uprising, and the civil unrest organized by the New Peoples' Army during the 1970s. All these had their origins partially in landlessness but just as significantly in absentee landlordism. According to both John Larkin's *The Pampangans* (1972) and Benedict Kerkvliet's *The Huk Rebellion* (1977), the paternalism of plantation owners diminished rapidly when they fled to the cities during the Japanese occupation. Class consciousness could be successfully appealed to, and then armed, only as the former familial relationship eroded. Indeed, class division has continued to increase as a result of postwar restrictions on land holdings, the sale of arable land for suburban development, reinvestment of subsequent profits in corporations clustered in highrise Makati, and the increasing importance of industrial over agricultural portions of the gross national product. In addition, ex-tenants following ex-landlords to the metropolis have found fewer opportunities for personal services and therefore for patronage.

Changes such as these have caused a decline in the simple

agrarian ideals that guaranteed cultural uniformity and stability. With diversification came a rise in expectations inadequately met by opportunities, so that large numbers of professionals who could not be absorbed by the Philippine economy or who preferred a meritocracy emigrated to the United States and Canada. After martial law was imposed late in 1972, political refugees swelled these numbers (Santos' novel-in-progress, *What the Hell For You Left Your Heart in San Francisco?*, uses material drawn from this group). Still more followed later, who considered regressive the autocratic rule of President/Premier Ferdinand Marcos and the rationalization of continuing "crisis government" under the guise of a New Society. By training, many of these later immigrants have been confident, self-possessed technicians, having little experience to share with earlier—and now older—Filipinos. Consequently, the "o.t.'s" (old-timers) may suffer from three kinds of distances at once: between themselves and their homeland; between themselves and their children who have known only America; and between themselves and recent arrivals whose Philippines, in some ways, is drastically different from their own.

Solomon King, in Santos' unpublished novel, *The Man Who (Thought He) Looked Like Robert Taylor*, feels bitterly this deterioration in the spirit of ethnic unity, which he himself will take to the grave. He has lived alone for thirty years in Chicago, surrounded by Poles and carefully preserved souvenirs of Sulucan where he was born and early orphaned. His father was a champion *arnis* fencer, using wooden weapons in "a silent duel of no touch." Solomon's life too has been spent in a kind of pantomime, so that he might pass unnoticed, untouched. But realizing that, like his idol Robert Taylor, he has not escaped the many little deaths that aging brings, he goes to Washington in search of whatever old friends may still be left. The lament of Solomon (a King Solomon less wise, and divided within himself) is played against a counterpoint of dialogues between anonymous Pinoys of his generation, at ease with one another but embarrassed by the better educated Filipinos now among them.

This new loneliness, this latest fear of no longer belonging to a culture which itself seems at times to be wasting away, finds expression in the rhythm of arrangement provided by the selections in *Scent of Apples*. "Immigration Blues" describes the still precarious situation of aliens and permanent residents, today. The segments of *You Lovely People* which follow are doubly retrospective, recovering incidents from Pinoy life during World War II, and folkways from a past even more remote. So receding a perspective could easily be considered nostalgic; or even elegiac; and the Pinoy characters, sentimentalists unable to adapt to the natural evolution of their dearest traditions. But the spiral motion of the final section makes it clear that Santos is offering an essentially timeless view of culture, which transcends history limited to the linear, the consecutive, and the one-dimensional.

Both "The Day the Dancers Came" and "The Contender" are contemporary accounts of how two old-timers, awkward before the beauty and surpassing sophistication of young travelers from home, recoil into one another's care for final comfort. They are poignant couples, but couples nonetheless. "Quicker with Arrows" is a tale of distraught Philippine-American lovers, in a roomful of opportunists who are planning how they will exploit the chaos in their country, just after the holocaust at Hiroshima. And in "Footnote to a Laundry List" a professor, recently returned from an ill-fated affair in the States, makes a sympathetic defense of a young female student, out of respect for what he remembers of love and innocence.

That this final sequence (present:present:remote past:recent past) is chronic, rather than chronological, suggests that Santos—throughout the entire collection—is less concerned with history perceived as ocean current or successive waves, than with culture as an entire archipelago of diverse islands in that stream. What he discerns is that any ethnic group consists of individual particles, no two of which are exactly identical (there are Filipinos, and Filipinos), but all of which have declared their commitment to participate, as if in some consummate entity. The declaration of a common bond, of course, tends to be more perfect than uneasy coexistence may actually turn out to be. Nevertheless, it provides a measure of meaning even for those who pay it lip service only.

This is the recurring theme in Santos' work: how hard it always is, yet how important, to be "Filipino" at heart, with all that that implies about human decency, good humor, and honor, consideration beyond courtesy, and putting both hands to a common burden; while at the same time trying to make a life out of being overseas Filipinos, Philippine-Americans, temporary "permanent residents" obligated to be buried "at home," or those assimilated beyond recovery of any heritage whatsoever.

As permeating as the scent of autumn apples is this single, persistent dream: the return of the Philippines to the man, whether or not a return to the Philippines is ever managed. Through dreams one presumes to distinguish the momentary from the momentous. For Santos, that ideal has too often been realized to be mocked as imaginary.

*Leonard Casper*

Boston College
March 1979

# PREFACE

*Each time I left the United States for the Philippines, I thought I* was going for good. In 1946, after an enforced stay of five wartime years, I returned to my family at the foot of Mount Mayon, vowing in my heart I would never leave home again. During the next dozen years, in memory of the Pinoys whose lives I shared, I wrote my first stories about Filipinos in America, later collected in *You Lovely People.* Then in 1958 I left for the States on a Rockefeller creative writing fellowship, "abandoning" a college presidency to which I had just been inaugurated. This time, however, I brought my wife, Beatriz, and ten-year-old son with me to Iowa City, where I enrolled in the Writers Workshop at the University of Iowa. It was here that I wrote my first novel, *Villa Magdalena,* and finished a draft of *The Volcano* on a 1960 Guggenheim fellowship. The following year we returned to the Philippines, passing through England, Ireland, Europe, and the Far East because, I thought, we might just as well see the world before finally settling down.

Both novels were published in 1965, the year I won the Republic Cultural Heritage Award in Literature. Of the many telegrams I received congratulating me, two came from men in government: one from the president of the Philippine Senate, Ferdinand Marcos; and the other from Senator Raul Manglapus, now an exile in this country from the Marcos martial law regime. Here perhaps is the kind of irony compounded of coincidence and fate that not only touches but quite completely alters, often scars without pity or reason, the lives of most Filipino exiles, particularly those in America, subject of all the stories in this book.

In 1966 I was in Iowa City again (with Beatriz, our son following us a year later) as Exchange Fulbright Professor in the Writers Workshop where I had once been a student. Three years later we returned to the Philippines, quite certain then that there would be no more going back to the States.

Seventeen years earlier, we had built what we called our dream house not far from the foot of the volcano, but we had not lived in it for more than a total of ten years, all told. We missed it as we did friends and kin and sensations like the now almost forgotten scent of calamondin fruit and papaya blossoms from trees which surrounded that house. So when we found ourselves back in Iowa in 1970, after less than a year of living in it, we carried a picture of the dream house that was still a dream in another, yet more poignant, sense. When friends dropped in for a visit to our apartment, usually on, or close to, a university campus, we showed them the picture as if to make up for the drabness of our surroundings and to underscore the fact that we were transients, not to mention the homesickness the gesture obviously implied.

Most of us Filipinos in this country keep albums of snapshots from home, which we show to one another without provocation, a ritual almost, like comparing hopes and wounds, like playing the roles I assigned to some of the characters in my stories. As a matter of fact, sometimes I cannot distinguish between these characters and the real persons I have known in America. The years have a way of distorting memories. Now, too, our coming and going appear to have taken the shape of my characters' predicaments. Like those who carry memories as a burden, I find it more and more impossible to travel light.

In the summer of 1972, Beatriz and I left Iowa to visit friends in Chicago, Detroit, and Toronto before flying home, this time definitely for good. We had been away too long. Now, whenever I opened a window in my dreams, on Washington Avenue or Riverside Park, I would see Mount Mayon looming over fields of coconut groves and banana trees, superimposed, in an incongruous double exposure, on a likeness of the Student Union or the First National Bank.

It was still summer when we arrived in San Francisco with plenty of time before the opening of classes for the second semester in the Philippines, where we were to assume our administrative jobs in the university from which we were both on extended leave. My novel, *The Praying Man*, was not scheduled for publication in Manila until December, maybe later. I was still at work on another novel, *The Man Who (Thought He) Looked Like Robert Taylor*. The days were mild and the nights, cooler than the autumns I had loved in the Midwest. The streets with names I could sing with the familiarity of old songs made me somehow feel at home. There were Filipinos everywhere, mostly old-timers who walked or sat around in the sun, on Union Street, in Chinatown, or close to the bay in the Sunset district where we lived. Sales day in the Emporium on Market Street was like Filipino day, a transplanted Quiapo or Central Market in Manila. There was time enough to stay on and write and once more live close to these people who have always been the subject of my fiction.

When in September we heard that martial law had been declared in the Philippines, we waited for further developments, but the news, instead of getting better, seemed to grow worse. *The Praying Man* became a casualty of martial law: it was disapproved for publication. No one knew when schools would reopen. In the conflicting news that came to us, one fact stood out clearly: the new political order was going to last a long time.

So we started looking for work to earn something to live on while waiting and hoping for better news from home. It was not easy. For some work we were willing to do, such as teaching in the elementary and junior high schools, we were considered overqualified. We were also told outright that we were too old. No doubt there was a youth cult in California. This has never been a country for the old. More reasons for going home, but we stayed.

We looked into every job possibility. In between trips for

job interviews outside the city as far away as San Luis Obispo, I started another novel, *What the Hell For You Left Your Heart in San Francisco,* which I wanted to be funny because these were sad times. Besides, there was enough light material in the lives of the Filipinos around, particularly among the new breed of Filipino immigrants, professionals and businessmen who lived in mansions on hills above the babel of the narrow streets, or in the exclusive residential sections away from the smell of the harbor and the fish markets. However, I could not forget the smell of decay and death in the apartments of the old-timers among my countrymen who sat out the evening of their lives before television sets in condemned buildings in downtown San Francisco. Then the grin in both story and writer kept getting twisted in a grimace of pain close to tears.

By the time I was appointed Distinguished Writer in Residence at Wichita State University, Kansas, in June 1973, I could not get back into the rhythm of my novel no matter how hard I tried. Meanwhile, other stories I had written about the Filipino in America were getting published in literary magazines and anthologies. When I received my copy of the *United States in Literature* (Scott, Foresman, 1979), I gave it to Beatriz with this dedication:

. . . as of now, it seems, I belong to the literature of two great countries: the Philippines, land of my birth; and the United States, sanctuary, a second home, to this exile I have somehow drawn you into.

Indeed, I seem to be drawing into this exile others close to me who, right now, are ready to come any time they can, just when my wife and I are thinking of going home. Oh, yes, for good, why not? All exiles want to go home. Many of the old Filipinos in the United States, as in these stories, never return, but in their imagination they make the journey a thousand times, taking the slowest boats because in their dreamworld time is not as urgent as actual time passing, quicker than arrows, kneading their flesh, crying on their bones. Some fool themselves into thinking that theirs is a voluntary exile, but it is not. The ones who stay here to die know this best. Their last thoughts are of childhood friends, of parents long dead, old loves, of familiar songs and dances, odors of home like sweat and sun on brown skin or scent of calamondin fruit and fresh papaya blossoms.

*Bienvenido N. Santos*

Wichita State University
Wichita, Kansas
April 1979

*SCENT OF APPLES*

# IMMIGRATION BLUES

*Through the window curtain, Alipio saw two women, one seemed* twice as large as the other. In their summer dresses, they looked like the country girls he knew back home in the Philippines, who went around peddling rice cakes. The slim one could have passed for his late wife Seniang's sister whom he remembered only in pictures because she never made it to the United States. Before Seniang's death, the couple had arranged for her coming to San Francisco, filing all the required petition papers to facilitate the approval of her visa. The sister was always "almost ready, all the papers have been signed," but she never showed up. His wife had been ailing and when she died, he thought that hearing of her death would hasten her coming, but the wire he had sent her was neither returned nor acknowledged.

The knocking on the door was gentle. A little hard of hearing, Alipio was not sure it was indeed a knocking on the door, but it sounded different from the little noises that sometimes hummed in his ears in the daytime. It was not yet noon, but it must be warm outside in all that sunshine, otherwise those two women would be wearing spring dresses at the least. There were summer days in San Francisco that were cold like winter in the Midwest.

He limped painfully to the door. Until last month, he wore crutches. The entire year before that, he was bed-ridden, but he had to force himself to walk about in the house after coming from the hospital. After Seniang's death, everything had

3

gone to pieces. It was one bust after another, he complained to the few friends who came to visit him.

"Seniang was my good luck. When God decided to take her, I had nothing but bad luck," he said.

Not long after Seniang's death, he was in a car accident. For almost a year he was in the hospital. The doctors were not sure he was going to walk again. He told them it was God's wish. As it was he was thankful he was still alive. It had been a horrible accident.

The case dragged on in court. His lawyer didn't seem too good about car accidents. He was an expert immigration lawyer, but he was a friend. As it turned out, Alipio lost the full privileges and benefits coming to him in another two years if he had not been hospitalized and had continued working until his official retirement.

However, he was well provided. He didn't spend a cent for doctor and medicine and hospital bills. Now there was the prospect of a few thousand dollars compensation. After deducting his lawyer's fees it would still be something to live on. He had social security benefits and a partial retirement pension. Not too bad, really. Besides, now he could walk a little although he still limped and had to move about with extreme care.

When he opened the door, the fat woman said, "Mr. Palma? Alipio Palma?" Her intonation sounded like the beginning of a familiar song.

"Yes," he said. "Come in, come on in." He had not talked to anyone the whole week. His telephone had not rung all that time, not even a wrong number, and there was nobody he wanted to talk to. The little noises in his ears had somehow kept him company. Radio and television sounds lulled him to sleep.

The thin one was completely out of sight as she stood behind the big one who was doing the talking. "I'm sorry, I should have phoned you first, but we were in a hurry."

"The house is a mess," Alipio said truthfully. Had he been imagining things? He remembered seeing two women on the porch. There was another one, who looked like Seniang's sister. The woman said "we," and just then the other one materialized, close behind the big one, who walked in with the assurance of a social worker, about to do him a favor.

"Sit down. Sit down. Anywhere," Alipio said as he led the two women through the dining room, past a huge rectangular table in the center. It was bare except for a vase of plastic flowers as centerpiece. He passed his hand over his face, a mannerism which Seniang hated. Like you have a hang-over, she chided him, and you can't see straight.

A TV set stood close to a wall in the small living room crowded with an assortment of chairs and tables. An aquarium crowded the mantelpiece of a fake fireplace. A lighted bulb inside the tank showed many colored fish swimming about in a haze of fish food. Some of it lay scattered on the edge of the shelf. The carpet underneath was sodden black. Old magazines and tabloids lay just about everywhere.

"Sorry to bother you like this," the fat one said as she plunked herself down on the nearest chair, which sagged to the floor under her weight. The thin one chose the end of the sofa away from the TV set.

"I was just preparing my lunch. I know it's quite early, but I had nothing to do," Alipio said, pushing down with both hands the seat of the cushioned chair near a moveable partition, which separated the living room from the dining room. "It's painful just trying to sit down. I'm not too well yet," he added as he finally made it.

"I hope we're not really bothering you," the fat one said. The other had not said a word. She looked pale and sick. Maybe she was hungry or cold.

"How's it outside?" Alipio asked. "I've not been out all day." Whenever he felt like it, he dragged a chair to the porch and sat there, watching the construction going on across the street and smiling at the people passing by who happened to look his way. Some smiled back and mumbled something like a greeting or a comment on the beauty of the day. He stayed on until he got bored or it became colder than he could stand.

"It's fine. It's fine outside. Just like Baguio," the fat one said.

"You know Baguio? I was born near there."

"We're sisters."

Alipio was thinking, won't the other one speak at all?

"I'm Mrs. Antonieta Zafra, the wife of Carlito. I believe you know him. He says you're friends. In Salinas back in the thirties. He used to be a cook at the Marina."

"Carlito, yes, yes, Carlito Zafra. We bummed together. We come from Ilocos. Where you from?"

"Aklan. My sister and I speak Cebuano."

"Oh, she speak? You, you don't speak Ilocano?"

"Not much. Carlito and I talk in English. Except when he's real mad, like when his cock don't fight or when he lose, then he speaks Ilocano. Cuss words. I've learned them myself. Some, anyway."

"Yes. Carlito. He love cockfighting. How's he?"

"Retired like you. We're now in Fresno. On a farm. He raises chickens and hogs. I do some sewing in town when I can. My sister here is Monica. She's older than me. Never been married."

Monica smiled at the old man, her face in anguish, as if near to tears.

"Carlito. He got some fighting cocks, I bet."

"Not anymore. But he talks a lot about cockfighting. But nobody, not even the pinoys and the Chicanos are interested in it." Mrs. Zafra appeared pleased at the state of things on her home front.

"I remember. Carlito once promoted a cockfight. Everything was ready, but the roosters won't fight. Poor man, he did everything to make them fight like having them peck on each other's necks and so forth. They were so tame, so friendly with each other. Only thing they didn't do is embrace." Alipio laughed, showing a set of perfectly white and even teeth, obviously dentures.

"He hasn't told me about that, I'll remind him."

"Do that. Where's he? Why isn't he with you?"

"We didn't know we'd find you. While visiting some friends this morning, we learned you live here." Mrs. Zafra was beaming on him.

"I've always lived here, but I got few friends now. So you're Mrs. Carlito. I thought he's dead already. I never hear from him. We're old now. We're old already when we got our citizenship papers right after Japanese surrender. So you and him. Good for Carlito."

"I heard about your accident."

"After Seniang died. She was not yet sixty, but she had this heart trouble. I took care of her." Alipio seemed to have forgotten his visitors. He sat there staring at the fish in the aquarium, his ears perked as though waiting for some sound, like the breaking of the surf not far away, or the TV set suddenly turned on.

The sisters looked at each other. Monica was fidgeting, her eyes seemed to say, let's go, let's get out of here.

"Did you hear that?" the old man said.

Monica turned to her sister, her eyes wild with panic. Mrs. Zafra leaned forward, her hand touching the edge of the chair where Alipio sat, and asked gently, "Hear what?"

"The waves. Listen. They're just outside, you know. The breakers have a nice sound like at home in the Philippines. We lived in a coastal town. Like here, I always tell Seniang, across that ocean is the Philippines, we're not far from home."

"But you're alone now. It's not good to be alone," Mrs. Zafra said.

"At night I hear better. I can see the Pacific Ocean from my bedroom. It sends me to sleep. I sleep soundly like I got no debts. I can sleep all day, too, but that's bad. So I walk. I walk much before. I go out there. I let the breakers touch me. It's nice the touch. Seniang always scold me, she says I'll be catching cold, but I don't catch cold, she catch the cold all the time."

"You must miss her," Mrs. Zafra said. Monica was staring at her hands on her lap while the sister talked. Monica's skin was transparent and the veins showed on the back of her hands like trapped eels.

"I take care of Seniang. I work all day and leave her here alone. When I come home, she's smiling. She's wearing my jacket and my slippers. You look funny, I says, why do you wear my things, you're lost inside them. She chuckles, you keep me warm all day, she says, like you're here, I smell you. Oh, that Seniang. You see, we have no baby. If we have a baby . . ."

"I think you and Carlito have the same fate. We have no baby also."

"God dictates," Alipio said, making an effort to stand. In a miraculous surge of power, Monica rushed to him and helped him up. She seemed astonished and embarrassed at what she had done.

"Thank you," said Alipio. "I have crutches, but I don't want no crutches. They tickle me, they hurt me, too." He watched Monica go back to her seat.

"You need help better than crutches," Mrs. Zafra said.

"God helps," Alipio said, walking towards the kitchen as if expecting to find the Almighty there.

Mrs. Zafra followed him. "What are you preparing?" she asked.

"Let's have lunch," he said, "I'm hungry. I hope you are also."

"We'll help you," Mrs. Zafra said, turning back to where Monica sat staring at her hands again and listening perhaps for the sound of the sea. She had not noticed nor heard her sister when she called, "Monica!"

The second time she heard her. Monica stood up and went to the kitchen.

"There's nothing to prepare," Alipio was saying, as he opened the refrigerator. "What you want to eat? Me, I don't eat bread so I got no bread. I eat rice. I was just opening a can of sardines when you come. I like sardines with lotsa tomato sauce, it's great with hot rice."

"Don't you cook the sardines?" Mrs. Zafra asked. "Monica will cook it for you if you want."

"No! If you cook sardines, it taste bad. Better uncooked. Besides it gets cooked on top of the hot rice. Mix with onions, chopped nice. Raw not cooked. You like it?"

"Monica loves raw onions, don't you, Sis?"

"Yes," Monica said in a low voice.

"Your sister, she is well?" Alipio said, glancing towards Monica.

Mrs. Zafra gave her sister an angry look.

"I'm okay," Monica said, a bit louder this time.

"She's not sick," Mrs. Zafra said, "But she's shy. Her own

shadow frightens her. I tell you, this sister of mine, she got problems."

"Oh?" Alipio exclaimed. He had been listening quite attentively.

"I eat onions, raw," Monica said. "Sardines, too, I like uncooked."

Her sister smiled. "What do you say, I run out for some groceries," she said, going back to the living room to get her bag.

"Thanks. But no need for you to do that. I got lotsa food, canned food. Only thing I haven't got is bread," Alipio said.

"I eat rice, too," Monica said.

Alipio reached up to open the cabinet. It was stacked full of canned food: corn beef, pork and beans, vienna sausage, tuna, crab meat, shrimp, chow mein, imitation noodles, and, of course, sardines, in green and yellow labels.

"The yellow ones with mustard sauce, not tomato," he explained.

"All I need is a cup of coffee," Mrs. Zafra said, throwing her handbag back on the chair in the living room.

Alipio opened two drawers near the refrigerator. "Look," he said as Mrs. Zafra came running back to the kitchen. "I got more food to last me . . . a long time."

The sisters gaped at the bags of rice, macaroni, spaghetti sticks, sugar, dried shrimps wrapped in cellophane, bottles of soy sauce and fish sauce, vinegar, ketchup, instant coffee, and more cans of sardines.

The sight of all that foodstuff seemed to have enlivened the old man. After all, food meant life, continuing sustenance, source of energy and health. "Now look here," he said, turning briskly now to the refrigerator, which he opened, the sudden light touching his face with a glow that erased years from his eyes. With a jerk he pulled open the large freezer, cramped full of meats. "Mostly lamb chops," he said, adding, "I like lamb chops."

"Carlito, he hates lamb chops," Mrs. Zafra said.

"I like lamb chops," Monica said, still wild eyed, but now a bit of color tinted her cheeks. "Why do you have so much food?" she asked.

Alipio looked at her before answering. He thought she

looked younger than Mrs. Zafra. "You see," he said, closing the refrigerator. He was beginning to chill. "I watch the papers for bargain sales. I can still drive the car when I feel right. It's only now my legs bothering me. So. I buy all I can. Save me many trips. Money, too."

Later they sat around the enormous table in the dining room. Monica shared half a plate of boiling rice topped with a sardine with Alipio. He showed her how to place the sardine on top, pressing it a little and pouring spoonfuls of tomato juice over it.

Mrs. Zafra had coffee and settled for a small can of vienna sausage and a little rice. She sipped her coffee meditatively.

"This is good coffee," she said. "I remember how we used to hoard Hills Bros. coffee at . . . at the convent. The sisters were quite selfish about it."

"Antonieta was a nun, a sister of mercy," Monica said.

"What?" Alipio exclaimed, pointing a finger at her for no apparent reason, an involuntary gesture of surprise.

"Yes, I was," Mrs. Zafra admitted. "When I married, I had been out of the order for more than a year, yes, in California, at St. Mary's."

"You didn't . . ." Alipio began.

"Of course not," she interrupted him. "If you mean did I leave the order to marry Carlito. Oh, no. He was already an old man when I met him."

"I see. We used to joke him because he didn't like the girls too much. He prefer the cocks." The memory delighted him so much, he reared his head up as he laughed, covering his mouth hastily, but too late. Some of the tomato soaked grains had already spilled out on his plate and on the table in front of him.

Monica looked pleased as she gathered carefully some of the grains on the table.

"He hasn't changed," Mrs. Zafra said vaguely. "It was me who wanted to marry him."

"You? After being a nun, you wanted to marry . . . Carlito? But why Carlito?" Alipio seemed to have forgotten for the moment that he was still eating. The steam from the rice touched his face till it glistened darkly. He was staring at Mrs. Zafra as he breathed in the aroma without savoring it.

"It's a long story," Mrs. Zafra said. She stabbed a chunky sausage and brought it to her mouth. She looked pensive as she chewed on it.

"When did this happen?"

"Five, six years ago. Six years ago, almost."

"That long?"

"She had to marry him," Monica said blandly.

"What?" Alipio shouted, visibly disturbed. There was the sound of dentures grating in his mouth. He passed a hand over his face. "Carlito done that to you?"

The coffee spilled a little as Mrs. Zafra put the cup down. "Why no," she said. "What are you thinking of?"

Before he could answer, Monica spoke in the same tone of voice, low, unexcited, saying, "He thinks Carlito got you pregnant, that's what."

"Carlito?" She turned to Monica in disbelief. "Why, Alipio knows Carlito," she said.

Monica shrugged her shoulders. "Why don't you tell him why?" she suggested.

"As I said, it's a long story, but I shall make it short," Mrs. Zafra began. She took a sip from her cup and continued, "After leaving the order, I couldn't find a job. I was interested in social work, but I didn't know anybody who could help me."

As she paused, Alipio said, "What the heck does Carlito know about social work?"

"Let me continue," Mrs. Zafra said.

She still had a little money, from home, and she was not too worried about being jobless. But there was the question of her status as an alien. Once out of the community, she was no longer entitled to stay in the United States, let alone secure employment. The immigration office began to hound her, as it did other Filipinos in similar predicaments. They were a pitiful lot. Some hid in the apartments of friends like criminals running away from the law. Of course, they were law breakers. Those with transportation money returned home, which they hated to do. At home they would be forced to invent stories, tell lies to explain away why they returned so soon. All their lives they had to learn how to cope with the stigma of failure in a foreign land. They were losers and no longer fit for anything useful. The more sensitive and weak lost their minds and had to be committed to insane asylums. Others became neurotic, antisocial, depressed in mind and spirit. Some turned to crime. Or just folded up, in a manner of speaking. It was a nightmare. Antonieta didn't want to go back to the Philippines under those circumstances. She would have had to be very convincing to prove that she was not thrown out of the order for immoral reasons. Just when she seemed to have reached the breaking point, she recalled incidents in which women in her situation married American citizens and, automatically, became entitled to permanent residency with an option to become U.S. citizens after five years. At first, she thought the idea of such a marriage was hideous, unspeakable. Perhaps other foreign women in similar situations, could do it—and have done it—but not Philippine girls. But what was so special about Philippine girls? Nothing really, but their upbringing was such that to place themselves in a situation where they had to tell a man that all they wanted was a marriage for convenience, was degrading, an unbearable shame. A form of self-destruction. Mortal sin. Better repatriation. A thousand times better.

When an immigration officer finally caught up with her, he proved to be very understanding and quite a gentleman. Yet he was firm. He was young, maybe of Italian descent, and looked like a salesman for a well-known company in the islands that dealt in farm equipment.

"I'm giving you one week," he said. "You have already overstayed by several months. If in one week's time, you haven't left yet, you might have to wait in jail for deportation proceedings."

She cried, oh, how she cried. She wished she had not left the order, no, not really. She had no regrets about leaving up to this point. Life in the convent had turned sour on her. She despised the sisters and the system, which she found tyrannical, inhuman. In her own way, she had a long series of talks with God and God had approved of the step she had taken. She was not going back to the order. Anyhow, even if she did, she would not be taken back. To jail then?

But why not marry an American citizen? In one week's time? How? Accost the first likely man and say, "You look like an American citizen. If you are, indeed, and you have the necessary papers to prove it, will you marry me? I want to remain in this country."

All week she talked to God. It was the same God she had worshipped and feared all her life. Now they were *palsy walsy*, on the best of terms. As she brooded over her misfortune, He brooded with her, sympathized with her, and finally advised her to go look for an elderly Filipino who was an American citizen, and tell him the truth of the matter. Tell him that if he wished, it could be a marriage in name only. For his trouble, she would be willing to pay. How much? If it's a bit too much, could she pay on the installment plan? If he wished . . . otherwise . . . Meanwhile He would look the other way.

How she found Carlito Zafra was another story, a much longer story, more confused and confusing. It was like a miracle, though. Her friend God could not have sent her to a better instrument to satisfy her need. That was not expressed well, but it amounted to that, a need. Carlito was an instrument necessary for her good. And, as it turned out, a not too unwilling instrument.

"We were married the day before the week was over," Mrs. Zafra said. "And I've been in this country ever since. And no regrets."

They lived well and simply, a country life. True, they were childless, but both of them were helping relatives in the Philippines, sending them money and goods marked Made in U.S.A.

"Lately, however, some of the goods we've been sending do not arrive intact. Do you know that some of the good quality material we send never reach our relatives? It's frustrating."

"We got lotsa thieves between here and there," Alipio said, but his mind seemed to be on something else.

"And I was able to send for Monica. From the snapshots she sent us she seemed to be getting thinner and more sickly, teaching in the barrio. And she wanted so much to come here."

"Seniang was like you also, hiding from immigration. I thank God for her," Alipio told Mrs. Zafra in such a low voice he could hardly be heard.

The sisters pretended they didn't know, but they knew practically everything about him. Alipio appeared tired, pensive, and eager to talk so they listened.

"She went to my apartment and said, without any hesitation, marry me and I'll take care of you. She was thin then and I thought what she said was funny, the others had been matching us, you know, but I was not really interested. I believe marriage mean children. And if you cannot produce children, why get married? Besides, I had ugly experiences, bad moments. When I first arrived in the States, here in Frisco, I was young and there were lotsa blondies hanging around on Kearny Street. It was easy. But I wanted a family and they didn't. None of 'em. So what the heck, I said."

Alipio realized that Seniang was not joking. She had to get married to an American citizen otherwise she would be deported. At that time, Alipio was beginning to feel the disadvantages of living alone. There was too much time in his hands. How he hated himself for some of the things he did. He believed that if he was married, he would be more sensible with his time and his money. He would be happier and live long. So when Seniang showed that she was serious, he agreed to marry her. It was not to be in name only. He wanted a woman. He liked her so much he would have proposed himself had he suspected that he had a chance. She was hard working, decent, and in those days, rather slim.

"Like Monica," he said.

"Oh, I'm thin," Monica protested, blushing deeply, "I'm all bones."

"Monica is my only sister. We have no brother," Mrs. Zafra said, adding more items to her sister's vita.

"Look," Monica said, "I finished everything on my plate. I've never tasted sardines this good. Especially the way you eat them. I'm afraid I've eaten up your lunch. This is my first full meal. And I thought I've lost my appetite already."

The words came out in a rush. It seemed she didn't want to stop and she paused only because she didn't know what else to say. She moved about, gaily and at ease, perfectly at home. Alipio watched her with a bemused look in his face as she gathered the dishes and brought them to the kitchen sink. When Alipio heard the water running, he stood up, without much effort this time, and walked to her saying, "Don't bother. I got all the time to do that. You got to leave me something to do. Come, perhaps your sister wants another cup of coffee."

Mrs. Zafra had not moved from her seat. She was watching the two argue about the dishes. When she heard Alipio mention coffee, she said, "No, no more, thanks. I've drunk enough to keep me awake all week."

"Well, I'm going to wash them myself later," Monica was saying as she walked back to the table, Alipio close behind her.

"You're an excellent host, Alipio." Mrs. Zafra spoke in a tone like a reading from a citation on a certificate of merit or something. "And to two complete strangers at that. You're a good man."

"But you're not strangers. Carlito is my friend. We were young together in this country. And that's something, you know. There are lotsa guys like us here. Old-timers, o.t.'s, they call us. Permanent residents. U.S. Citizens. We all gonna be buried here." He appeared to be thinking deeply as he added, "But what's wrong about that?"

The sisters ignored the question. The old man was talking to himself.

"What's wrong is to be dishonest. Earn a living with both hands, not afraid of any kind of work, that's the best good. No other way. Yes, everything for convenience, why not? That's frankly honest. No pretend. Love comes in the afterwards. When it comes. If it comes."

Mrs. Zafra chuckled, saying, "Ah, you're a romantic, Alipio. I must ask Carlito about you. You seem to know so much about him. I bet you were quite a . . ." she paused because what she wanted to say was "rooster," but she might give the impression of over-familiarity.

Alipio interrupted her, saying, "Ask him, he will say yes, I'm a romantic." His voice held a vibrance that was a surprise and a revelation to the visitors. He gestured as he talked, puckering his mouth every now and then, obviously to keep his dentures from slipping out. "What do you think? We were young, why not? We wowed 'em with our gallantry, with our cooking. Boy those dames never seen anything like us. Also, we were fools, most of us, anyway. Fools on fire."

Mrs. Zafra clapped her hands. Monica was smiling.

"Ah, but that fire's gone. Only the fool's left now," Alipio said, weakly. His voice was low and he looked tired as he passed both hands across his face. Then he raised his head. The listening look came back to his face. When he spoke, his voice shook a little.

"Many times I wonder where are the others. Where are you? Speak to me. And I think they're wondering the same, asking the same, so I say, I'm here, your friend Alipio Palma, my leg is broken, the wife she's dead, but I'm okay. Are you okay also? The dead they can hear even if they don't answer. The alive don't answer. But I know. I feel. Some okay, some not. They old now, all of us, who were very young. All over the United States of America. All over the world . . ."

Abruptly, he turned to Mrs. Zafra, saying, "So. You and Carlito. But Carlito, he never had fire."

"How true, how very very true," Mrs. Zafra laughed. "It would burn him. Can't stand it. Not Carlito. But he's a good man, I can tell you that."

"No question. Dabest," Alipio conceded.

Monica remained silent, but her eyes followed every move Alipio made, straying no further than the reach of his arms as he gestured to help make clear the intensity of his feeling.

"I'm sure you still got some of that fire," Mrs. Zafra said.

Monica gasped, but she recovered quickly. Again a rush of words came from her lips as if they had been there all the time waiting for what her sister had said that touched off the torrent of words. Her eyes shone as in a fever as she talked.

"I don't know Carlito very well. I've not been with them very long, but from what you say, from the way you talk, from what I see, the two of you are very different."

"Oh, maybe not," Alipio said, trying to protest, but Monica went on.

"You have strength, Mr. Palma. Strength of character. Strength in your belief in God. I admire that in a man, in a human being. Look at you. Alone. This huge table. Don't you find it too big sometimes?" Monica paused perhaps to allow her meaning to sink into Alipio's consciousness, as she fixed her eyes on him.

"No, not really. I don't eat at this table. I eat in the kitchen," Alipio said.

Mrs. Zafra was going to say something, but she held back. Monica was talking again.

"But it must be hard, that you cannot deny. Living from day to day. Alone. On what? Memories? Cabinets and a refrigerator full of food? I repeat, I admire you, sir. You've found your place. You're home safe. And at peace." She paused again this time to sweep back the strand of hair that had fallen on her brow.

Alipio had a drugged look. He seemed to have lost the drift of her speech. What was she talking about? Groceries? Baseball? He was going to say, you like baseball also? You like tuna? I have all kinds of fish. Get them at bargain price. But, obviously, it was not the proper thing to say.

"Well, I guess, one gets used to anything. Even loneliness," Monica said in a listless, dispirited tone, all the fever in her voice gone.

"God dictates," Alipio said, feeling he had found his way again and he was now on the right track. What a girl. If she had only a little more flesh. And color.

Monica leaned back on her chair, exhausted. Mrs. Zafra was staring at her in disbelief, in grievous disappointment. Her eyes seemed to say, what happened, you were going great, what suddenly hit you that you had to stop, give up, defeated? Monica shook her head in a gesture that quite clearly said, no, I can't do it, I can't anymore, I give up.

Their eyes kept up a show, a deaf-mute dialogue. Mrs. Zafra: Just when everything was going on fine, you quit. We've reached this far and you quit. I could have done it my way, directly, honestly. Not that what you were doing was dishonest, you were great, and now look at that dumb expression in your eyes. Monica: I can't. I can't anymore. But I tried. It's too much.

"How long have you been in the States?" Alipio asked Monica.

"For almost a year now!" Mrs. Zafra screamed and Alipio was visibly shaken, but she didn't care. This was the right moment. She would take it from here whether Monica went along with her or not. She was going to do it her way. "How long exactly, let's see. Moni, when did you get your last extension?"

"Extension?" Alipio repeated the word. It had such a familiar ring like "visa" or "social security," it broke into his consciousness like a touch from Seniang's fingers. It was quite intimate. "You mean . . ."

"That's right. She's here as a temporary visitor. As a matter of fact, she came on a tourist visa. Carlito and I sponsored her coming, filed all the necessary papers, and everything would have been fine, but she couldn't wait. She had to come here as a tourist. Now she's in trouble."

"What trouble?" Alipio asked.

"She has to go back to the Philippines. She can't stay here any longer."

"I have only two days left," Monica said, her head in her hands. "And I don't want to go back."

Alipio glanced at the wall clock. It was past three. They had been talking for hours. It was visas right from the start. Marriages. The long years and the o.t.'s Now it was visas again. Were his ears playing a game? They might as well as they did sometimes, but his eyes surely were not. He could see this woman very plainly, sobbing on the table. Boy, she was in big trouble. Visas. Immigration. Boy, oh, boy! He knew all about that. His gleaming dentures showed a crooked smile. He turned to Mrs. Zafra.

"Did you come here," he began, but Mrs. Zafra interrupted him.

"Yes, Alipio. Forgive us. As soon as we arrived, I wanted to tell you without much talk, I wanted to say, 'I must tell you why we're here. I've heard about you. Not only from Carlito, but from other Filipinos who know you, how you're living here in San Francisco alone, a widower, and we heard of the accident, your stay in the hospital, when you were released, everything. Here's my sister, a teacher in the Philippines, never married, worried to death because she's being deported unless something turned up like she could marry a U.S. citizen, like I did, like your late wife Seniang, like many others have done, are doing in this exact moment, who can say? Now look at her, she's good, religious, any arrangement you wish, she'd accept it.' But I didn't have a chance to say it. You welcomed us like old friends, relatives. Later every time I began to say something about why we came, she interrupted me. I was afraid she had changed her mind and then she began to talk, then stopped without finishing what she really wanted to say, that is, why we came to see you, and so forth."

"No, no!" Monica cried, raising her head, her eyes red from weeping, her face damp with tears. "You're such a good man. We couldn't do this to you. We're wrong. We started wrong. We should've been more honest, but I was ashamed. I was afraid. Let's go! let's go!"

"Where you going?" Alipio asked.

"Anywhere," Monica answered. "Forgive us. Forgive me, Mister. Alipio, please."

"What's to forgive? Don't go. We have dinner. But first, let's have *merienda*. I take *merienda*. You do also, don't you? And I don't mean snacks like the Americans."

The sisters exchanged glances, their eyes chattering away.

Alipio chuckled. He wanted to say, talk of lightning striking same fellow twice, but thought better of it. A bad thing to say. Seniang was not lightning. At times only. Mostly his fault. And this girl Monica . . . Moni? Nice name also. How can this one be lightning?

Mrs. Zafra picked up her purse and before anyone could stop her, she was opening the door. "Where's the nearest grocery store around here?" she asked, but she didn't wait for an answer.

"Come back, come back here, we got lotsa food," Alipio called after her, but he might just as well have been calling the Pacific Ocean.

Mrs. Zafra took time although a supermarket was only a few blocks away. When she returned, her arms were full of groceries in paper bags. Alipio and Monica met her on the porch.

"*Comusta?*" she asked, speaking in the dialect for the first time as Monica relieved her of her load. The one word question seemed to mean much more than "How are you?" or "How has it been?"

Alipio replied in English. "God dictates," he said, his dentures sounding faintly as he smacked his lips, but he was not looking at the foodstuff in the paper bags Monica was carrying. His eyes were on her legs, in the direction she was taking. She knew where the kitchen was, of course. He just wanted to be sure she won't lose her way. Like him. On his way to the kitchen, sometimes he found himself in the bedroom. Lotsa things happened to men his age.

# SCENT OF APPLES

*When I arrived in Kalamazoo it was October and the war was still* on. Gold and silver stars hung on pennants above silent windows of white and brick-red cottages. In a backyard an old man burned leaves and twigs while a grey-haired woman sat on the porch, her red hands quiet on her lap, watching the smoke rising above the elms, both of them thinking of the same thought perhaps, about a tall, grinning boy with blue eyes and flying hair, who went out to war: where could he be now this month when leaves were turning into gold and the fragrance of gathered apples was in the wind?

It was a cold night when I left my room at the hotel for a usual speaking engagement. I walked but a little way. A heavy wind coming up from Lake Michigan was icy on the face. It felt like winter straying early in the northern woodlands. Under the lampposts the leaves shone like bronze. And they rolled on the pavements like the ghost feet of a thousand autumns long dead, long before the boys left for faraway lands without great icy winds and promise of winter early in the air, lands without apple trees, *the singing and the gold!*

It was the same night I met Celestino Fabia, "just a Filipino farmer" as he called himself, who had a farm about thirty miles east of Kalamazoo.

"You came all that way on a night like this just to hear me talk?" I asked.

"I've seen no Filipino for so many years now," he answered quickly. "So when I saw your name in the papers where it says you come from the Islands and that you're going to talk, I come right away."

Earlier that night I had addressed a college crowd, mostly women. It appeared that they wanted me to talk about my country; they wanted me to tell them things about it because my country had become a lost country. Everywhere in the land the enemy stalked. Over it a great silence hung; and their boys were there, unheard from, or they were on their way to some little known island on the Pacific, young boys all, hardly men, thinking of harvest moons and smell of forest fire.

It was not hard talking about our own people. I knew them well and I loved them. And they seemed so far away during those terrible years that I must have spoken of them with a little fervor, a little nostalgia.

In the open forum that followed, the audience wanted to know whether there was much difference between our women and the American women. I tried to answer the question as best as I could, saying, among other things, that I did not know much about American women, except that they looked friendly, but differences or similarities in inner qualities such as naturally belonged to the heart or to the mind, I could only speak about with vagueness.

While I was trying to explain away the fact that it was not easy to make comparisons, a man rose from the rear of the hall, wanting to say something. In the distance, he looked slight and old and very brown. Even before he spoke, I knew that he was, like me, a Filipino.

"I'm a Filipino," he began, loud and clear, in a voice that seemed used to wide open spaces, "I'm just a Filipino farmer out in the country." He waved his hand towards the door. "I left the Philippines more than twenty years ago and have never been back. Never will perhaps. I want to find out, sir, are our Filipino women the same like they were twenty years ago?"

As he sat down, the hall filled with voices, hushed and intrigued. I weighed my answer carefully. I did not want to tell a lie yet I did not want to say anything that would seem platitudinous, insincere. But more important than these considerations, it seemed to me that moment as I looked towards my countryman, I must give him an answer that would not make him so unhappy. Surely, all these years, he must have held on to certain ideals, certain beliefs, even illusions peculiar to the exile.

"First," I said as the voices gradually died down and every eye seemed upon me, "First, tell me what our women were like twenty years ago."

The man stood to answer. "Yes," he said, "you're too young . . . Twenty years ago our women were nice, they were modest, they wore their hair long, they dressed proper and went for no monkey business. They were natural, they went to church regular, and they were faithful." He had spoken slowly, and now in what seemed like an afterthought, added, "It's the men who ain't."

Now I knew what I was going to say.

"Well," I began, "it will interest you to know that our women have changed—but definitely! The change, however, has been on the outside only. Inside, here," pointing to the heart, "they are the same as they were twenty years ago God-fearing, faithful, modest, and *nice*."

The man was visibly moved. "I'm very happy, sir," he said, in the manner of one who, having stakes on the land, had found no cause to regret one's sentimental investment.

After this, everything that was said and done in that hall that night seemed like an anti-climax; and later, as we walked outside, he gave me his name and told me of his farm thirty miles east of the city.

We had stopped at the main entrance to the hotel lobby. We had not talked very much on the way. As a matter of fact, we were never alone. Kindly American friends talked to us, asked us questions, said goodnight. So now I asked him whether he cared to step into the lobby with me and talk.

"No, thank you," he said, "you are tired. And I don't want to stay out too late."

"Yes, you live very far."

"I got a car," he said, "besides . . ."

Now he smiled, he truly smiled. All night I had been watching his face and I wondered when he was going to smile.

"Will you do me a favor, please," he continued smiling almost sweetly. "I want you to have dinner with my family out in the country. I'd call for you tomorrow afternoon, then drive you back. Will that be all right?"

"Of course," I said. "I'd love to meet your family." I was leaving Kalamazoo for Muncie, Indiana, in two days. There was plenty of time.

"You will make my wife very happy," he said.

"You flatter me."

"Honest. She'll be very happy. Ruth is a country girl and hasn't met many Filipinos. I mean Filipinos younger than I, cleaner looking. We're just poor farmer folk, you know, and we don't get to town very often. Roger, that's my boy, he goes to school in town. A bus takes him early in the morning and he's back in the afternoon. He's nice boy."

"I bet he is," I agreed. "I've seen the children of some of the boys by their American wives and the boys are tall, taller than the father, and very good looking."

"Roger, he'd be tall. You'll like him."

Then he said goodbye and I waved to him as he disappeared in the darkness.

The next day he came, at about three in the afternoon. There was a mild, ineffectual sun shining; and it was not too cold. He was wearing an old brown tweed jacket and worsted trousers to match. His shoes were polished, and although the green of his tie seemed faded, a colored shirt hardly accentuated it. He looked younger than he appeared the night before now that he was clean shaven and seemed ready to go to a party. He was grinning as we met.

"Oh, Ruth can't believe it. She can't believe it," he kept repeating as he led me to his car—a nondescript thing in faded black that had known better days and many hands. "I says to her, I'm bringing you a first class Filipino, and she says, aw, go away, quit kidding, there's no such thing as first class Filipino. But Roger, that's my boy, he believed me immediately. What's he like, daddy, he asks. Oh, you will see, I says, he's first class. Like you daddy? No, no, I laugh at him, your daddy ain't first class. Aw, but you are, daddy, he says. So you can see what a nice boy he is, so innocent. Then Ruth starts griping about the house, but the house is a mess, she says. True it's a mess, it's always a mess, but you don't mind, do you? We're poor folks, you know."

The trip seemed interminable. We passed through narrow lanes and disappeared into thickets, and came out on barren land overgrown with weeds in places. All around were dead leaves and dry earth. In the distance were apple trees.

"Aren't those apple trees?" I asked wanting to be sure.

"Yes, those are apple trees," he replied. "Do you like apples? I got lots of 'em. I got an apple orchard, I'll show you."

All the beauty of the afternoon seemed in the distance, on the hills, in the dull soft sky.

"Those trees are beautiful on the hills," I said.

"Autumn's a lovely season. The trees are getting ready to die, and they show their colors, proud-like."

"No such thing in our own country," I said.

That remark seemed unkind, I realized later. It touched him off on a long deserted tangent, but ever there perhaps. How many times did the lonely mind take unpleasant detours away from the familiar winding lanes towards home for fear of this, the remembered hurt, the long lost youth, the grim shadows of the years; how many times indeed, only the exile knows.

It was a rugged road we were travelling and the car made so much noise that I could not hear everything he said, but I understood him. He was telling his story for the first time in many years. He was remembering his own youth. He was thinking of home. In these odd moments there seemed no cause for fear no cause at all, no pain. That would come later. In the night perhaps. Or lonely on the farm under the apple trees.

*In this old Visayan town, the streets are narrow and dirty and strewn with corral shells. You have been there? You could not have missed our house, it was the biggest in town, one of the oldest, ours was a big family. The house stood right on the edge of the street. A door opened heavily and you enter a dark hall leading to the stairs. There is the smell of chickens roosting on the low-topped walls, there is the familiar sound they make and you grope your way up a massive staircase, the bannisters smooth upon the trembling hand. Such nights, they are no better than the days, windows are closed against the sun; they close heavily.*

*Mother sits in her corner looking very white and sick. This was her world, her domain. In all these years I cannot remember the sound of her voice. Father was different. He moved about. He shouted. He ranted. He lived in the past and talked of honor as though it were the only thing.*

*I was born in that house. I grew up there into a pampered brat. I was mean. One day I broke their hearts. I saw mother cry wordlessly as father heaped his curses upon me and drove me out of the house, the gate closing heavily after me. And my brothers and sisters took up my father's hate for me and multiplied it numberless times in their own broken hearts. I was no good.*

*But sometimes, you know, I miss that house, the roosting chickens on the low-topped walls. I miss my brothers and sisters. Mother sitting in her chair, looking like a pale ghost in a corner of the room. I would remember the great live posts, massive tree trunks from the forests. Leafy plants grew on the sides, buds pointing downwards, wilted and died before they could become flowers. As they fell on the floor, father bent to pick them and throw them out into the corral streets. His hands were strong. I have kissed those hands . . . many times, many times.*

Finally we rounded a deep curve and suddenly came upon a shanty, all but ready to crumble in a heap on the ground, its plastered walls were rotting away, the floor was hardly a foot from the ground. I thought of the cottages of the poor colored folk in the south, the hovels of the poor everywhere in the land. This one stood all by itself as though by common consent all the folk that used to live here had decided to stay away, despising it, ashamed of it. Even the lovely season could not color it with beauty.

A dog barked loudly as we approached. A fat blonde woman stood at the door with a little boy by her side. Roger seemed newly scrubbed. He hardly took his eyes off me. Ruth had a clean apron around her shapeless waist. Now as she shook my hands in sincere delight I noticed shamefacedly (that I should notice) how rough her hands, how coarse and red with labor, how ugly! She was no longer young and her smile was pathetic.

As we stepped inside and the door closed behind us, immediately I was aware of the familiar scent of apples. The room

was bare except for a few ancient pieces of second-hand furni-
ture. In the middle of the room stood a stove to keep the family warm in winter. The walls were bare. Over the dining table
hung a lamp yet unlighted.

Ruth got busy with the drinks. She kept coming in and out
of a rear room that must have been the kitchen and soon the
table was heavy with food, fried chicken legs and rice, and
green peas and corn on the ear. Even as we ate, Ruth kept
standing, and going to the kitchen for more food. Roger ate
like a little gentleman.

"Isn't he nice looking?" his father asked.

"You are a handsome boy, Roger," I said.

The boy smiled at me. "You look like Daddy," he said.

Afterwards I noticed an old picture leaning on the top of a
dresser and stood to pick it up. It was yellow and soiled with
many fingerings. The faded figure of a woman in Philippine
dress could yet be distinguished although the face had become
a blur.

"Your . . ." I began.

"I don't know who she is," Fabia hastened to say. "I picked
that picture many years ago in a room on La Salle Street in
Chicago. I have often wondered who she is."

"The face wasn't a blur in the beginning?"

"Oh, no. It was a young face and good."

Ruth came with a plate full of apples.

"Ah," I cried, picking out a ripe one, "I've been thinking
where all the scent of apples came from. The room is full of it."

"I'll show you," said Fabia.

He showed me a backroom, not very big. It was half-full of
apples.

"Every day," he explained, "I take some of them to town to
sell to the groceries. Prices have been low. I've been losing on
the trips."

"These apples will spoil," I said.

"We'll feed them to the pigs."

Then he showed me around the farm. It was twilight now
and the apple trees stood bare against a glowing western sky.
In apple blossom time it must be lovely here, I thought. But
what about wintertime?

One day, according to Fabia, a few years ago, before Roger was born, he had an attack of acute appendicitis. It was deep winter. The snow lay heavy everywhere. Ruth was pregnant and none too well herself. At first she did not know what to do. She bundled him in warm clothing and put him on a cot near the stove. She shoveled the snow from their front door and practically carried the suffering man on her shoulders, dragging him through the newly made path towards the road where they waited for the U.S. Mail car to pass. Meanwhile snowflakes poured all over them and she kept rubbing the man's arms and legs as she herself nearly froze to death.

"Go back to the house, Ruth!" her husband cried, "you'll freeze to death."

But she clung to him wordlessly. Even as she massaged his arms and legs, her tears rolled down her cheeks. "I won't leave you, I won't leave you," she repeated.

Finally the U.S. Mail car arrived. The mailman, who knew them well, helped them board the car, and, without stopping on his usual route, took the sick man and his wife direct to the nearest hospital.

Ruth stayed in the hospital with Fabia. She slept in a corridor outside the patients' ward and in the day time helped in scrubbing the floor and washing the dishes and cleaning the men's things. They didn't have enough money and Ruth was willing to work like a slave.

"Ruth's a nice girl," said Fabia, "like our own Filipino women."

Before nightfall, he took me back to the hotel. Ruth and Roger stood at the door holding hands and smiling at me. From inside the room of the shanty, a low light flickered. I had a last glimpse of the apple trees in the orchard under the darkened sky as Fabia backed up the car. And soon we were on our way back to town. The dog had started barking. We could hear it for some time, until finally, we could not hear it anymore, and all was darkness around us, except where the head lamps revealed a stretch of road leading somewhere.

Fabia did not talk this time. I didn't seem to have anything to say myself. But when finally we came to the hotel and I got down, Fabia said, "Well, I guess I won't be seeing you again."

It was dimly lighted in front of the hotel and I could hardly see Fabia's face. Without getting off the car, he moved to where I had sat, and I saw him extend his hand. I gripped it.

"Tell Ruth and Roger," I said, "I love them."

He dropped my hand quickly. "They'll be waiting for me now," he said.

"Look," I said, not knowing why I said it, "one of these days, very soon, I hope, I'll be going home. I could go to your town."

"No," he said softly, sounding very much defeated but brave, "Thanks a lot. But, you see, nobody would remember me now."

Then he started the car, and as it moved away, he waved his hand.

"Goodbye," I said, waving back into the darkness. And suddenly the night was cold like winter straying early in these northern woodlands.

I hurried inside. There was a train the next morning that left for Muncie, Indiana, at a quarter after eight.

# AND BEYOND, MORE WALLS

*I came to New York to see the Statue of Liberty and my cousin* Manuel who left the Philippines sixteen years ago. At the International House there was no room for me. Summer classes had started and the House was full. My plea, "I'm a Filipino," didn't do me any good. Corregidor had fallen long ago and *Life* magazine had a picture of General Wainwright surrendering to the Japs at Bataan, and there was another picture of my little countrymen advancing toward the enemy with white banners flying.

So I stayed in a hotel that night. It was hot, like summer in the Philippines. The elevated roared across my pillow through my brain and all night I lay awake in the dark thinking of home and my childhood, of the railroads beyond the whitewashed walls, trains running far into the night for near and far off places.

In the other room, at right angle to mine, a white woman was lying on the bed, reading under the lamp light, and I wondered if she had already seen the Statue of Liberty.

I had not, but I had already seen my cousin Manuel.

It was midsummer when I saw him and it was hot like the first night I came to New York and could not sleep. When I finally located his apartment it was already night, but the sun was still shining over the Hudson. I was excited to see him after these many years.

He knew I was coming. "Come over the earliest time you

30

can," he had said over the phone. I wanted to believe there was eagerness in his voice.

I knocked on the door of his room and waited. What did he look like now? What would I say to him? Should I tell him that his mother was dead, that his only brother was in the Sanatorium when I left the Philippines? I knocked on the door again.

"Who izzit?" sounded the voice from the room. Strange that I knew it was his voice. This was more familiar than the voice I heard over the phone.

"This is Ben," I said, putting my ear to the door, eager for another sound of his voice. Manuel and I were like brothers although he was older than I.

The door opened slowly. "Ben!" he cried, pulling me inside the room and closing the door after me.

We embraced, and I tried to cry out his name, but there was a choking in my throat. He gave me a chair and I looked around and saw a girl sitting on the bed, playing cards.

It was a small, stuffy room, smaller than the room I occupied in the hotel. There were curtains on what looked like windows, a wooden table and two chairs, and an ice box near a little closed door. Through those windows was a circular court where the grass was withered, and beyond, more walls.

Manuel looked the same, exactly as I thought he would look. Tall and slim. He was wearing a silk blue shirt that matched the light blue of his cuffless trousers. He wore a gold wrist watch. He smiled at me.

"You have not changed," he said, above the sound of the radio on a small table by the bed.

"Turn that off," he said, and the girl turned the radio low. She was radiantly white and thin.

"Oh," said Manuel as if remembering there was another person in the room, "this is Helen. Helen, this is Ben, my cousin."

Helen turned toward me and smiled. Her teeth were not as her lips had promised.

"Jesus! it's beastly hot tonight," said Manuel as he walked toward the ice box, and opened it, peering inside, "Well, well, who would think of it, after sixteen years, we meet in New York."

I chuckled. Manuel has not changed, I repeated to myself. His thick lips forever smiling. His eyes black and deep like my mother's.

"How do you like America?" Manuel asked, putting the beer bottles on the table.

"You mean New York?" I asked.

"America—just the same."

"It's fine."

Looking at him, I thought he was much better looking than his brother in the Sanatorium. Manuel had such a young face, he could pass for less than his thirty-five years.

"How did you live through the winter?" he asked. "Was it cold out there in the Midwest?"

He spoke like an American, very fluently. I was ashamed of my accent.

He placed empty glasses on the table, saying how cold it could be sometimes in New York. A Negro voice moaned over the radio, as if the singer were singing a farewell before death.

From where we sat, my back was toward the girl, but whenever I looked at the mirror over the dresser, I could see her, shuffling the cards, laying them out on the bed.

"Shall we drink?" Manuel asked, and I shook my head.

He laughed softly and peered again into the ice box. "You should learn how to drink, Ben. This is America," he said.

Placing soft drinks on the table, he opened a bottle for me and poured into my glass.

"I like beer," he said after a while, opening a bottle.

The cold drink was nice to my parched throat, and I nearly finished the whole glass.

"Darn good that drink," he said, pointing to my glass, "But there's no kick to it."

"Give me a bottle," said Helen.

"Help yourself," he answered, looking at me fondly. For sometime there were no words spoken, only the singing from the radio, and the clatter of the tin bottle cap on the floor after Helen had opened a bottle. She went back to her cards.

"Well," I said, not knowing what to say.

"What did you feel after Pearl Harbor?"

"I wanted to stop studying."

He shook his head. "Bad times. I bet you have cried a lot since then."

I admitted it. "Haven't you?" I asked.

"After sixteen years, Ben, you can't cry no more."

The walls were bare except for a small framed painting in watercolor, a reproduction of a scene in Venice.

"That's not mine," Manuel explained, pointing at the picture with his glass. "That was there when I took this room. Funny, in the beginning I carried the pictures of Father and Mother and my brother Berto in my pocketbook, and had an enlargement made of them. Framed them in style, and placed them on my dresser. I looked at them when I was feeling kind of homesick, but heck, a man can't keep doing that for sixteen years without going nuts."

There was a picture of Manuel on the dresser, his arm around a plump American girl in a bathing suit.

"When was the last time you wrote home?" I asked.

"Let's see . . . Five years ago . . . More or less."

"I know," I said. "Suddenly our folks didn't know where you were. Why did you stop writing them?"

"Well, I guess I had nothing more to say. Surprised?"

"No," I managed to say. I did not tell him: Manuel, I was around when your mother died. She had a hard time dying. Cancer. People said it was because of you, that she was waiting to see you before she died. And when I left Manila, I saw Berto in the Sanatorium, looking like a skeleton. See him for me, Berto said, and give him my love.

"What's the matter?" asked Manuel.

"Nothing," I answered, wiping my face. "It's hot around here."

"I suppose," he said as if he had not heard me, "I have to ask, how's Father, Mother, how's Berto? And maybe you have sad news to tell. Go ahead, Ben. I can take it, don't you think I can? Suppose they are all dead, what of it? Suppose they are still living, so what? For all we know, it may be worse for them now living than dead." He paused, as if he had all of a sudden become very tired. After a while, he added, "C'mon, try this beer, it won't hurt you, son."

A radio voice was crooning:

> *The shepherds will tend the sheep*
> *The valley will bloom again . . .*

"Oh, yes," Manuel said, "in one of their last letters I got, they mentioned a terrible storm."

"That was long ago, five or six years ago. Terrible storm indeed. Swept the whole town. There was a flood, too. Left sand on our rice fields. Many houses were blown down, but your house withstood the typhoon."

He looked sleepy, but now he brightened up. "Good ol' house," waving his hand in tribute. "Those big round posts, thick hard wooden walls. That house will stand forever. And that's a fact. Do you know how old it is? About a hundred years old. No kiddin'. Lots of people have lived and died there. Pretty soon, there will be nothing in that ol' good house but ghosts, and mine will not be one of them either . . . no, sir!" He shook his head.

Then I saw a bellhop's uniform hanging near the wash room. Manuel saw me looking at it, and he laughed. "A ghost in a bellhop's uniform, that's rich!"

And he wanted some more beer, but there was no more beer.

"Darn it!" he said.

The soft drink in my glass was no longer cold and there was no air in the room, it seemed.

"Yep, yep," Manuel muttered under his breath, looking into his empty glass, "Darn good ol' house. Stronger than the church. You know our great grandfather was richer than the church, but . . ."

"The church roof was blown down," I said.

"You don't say! Well, for heaven's sake! What did the ol' *padre* and his . . . say, we were servers in that church on weekends, remember?"

I smiled, remembering. My cousin started laughing, very loudly this time, and the girl in the mirror looked at him.

"Did that *padre* ever know," he laughed, "I always tasted the wine ahead of him? Maybe I owe the ol' *padre* my excellent taste for drinks."

The girl bent toward the radio and the song drowned Manuel's unholy laughter—clap, clapping of hands, deep in the heart of Texas!

Involuntarily, my cousin started beating to the rhythm. .

There was a newspaper lying on the floor at my feet, and I stooped, trying to read the headlines.

"What's your draft classification?" Manuel asked, standing beside me.

"II-A. Deferred until further notice on account of my studies. How about you?"

"Me? I'm great!" He bent his head with a flourish as if he were a courtier before a grand lady, "Greetings to Manuel Buenavista, from the President of the United States . . ." and relaxing, added in his natural voice, "I'll soon be inducted, you know."

"How do you like it?"

"I love it. I'm going to die for my country!" He tried to mimic a soap box orator.

"He's crazy," said Helen.

"Shut up! I'm going to die for my country," he said and then paused dramatically, as if he had forgotten his lines, "Hell, what's my country? Remember what we used to sing in school?"

And he sang:

> *My country 'tis of thee*
> *Sweet land of Liberty,*
> *Of thee I sing.*

"You're nuts!" said Helen, "that's America."

"What d'ye think it was, *One Dozen Roses?* . . . Boy those songs we sang in school! We don't hear the likes of them these days. Then our school programs . . ."

It continued oppressively warm in the room, but Manuel's reminiscing was contaminating. I remembered Manuel was the only kid in town who played the violin. He used to say he would be a great violinist.

"You took your violin with you, didn't you, Manuel?" I asked.

"Yep, I did. But what good did it do me? Like a mouse—yes, I was like a mouse—I lived from hole to hole, hellish dumps like this, and every time I thought I'd found a place where I could play it, my neighbors raised hell, knocked on the walls and called me names . . . how d'ye like that?"

"Maybe you played lousy," said Helen, without looking at him. She was still playing solitaire.

"I did not! Ask Ben . . . what do you say. Ben? . . . Or suppose I did, what the hell? All that mattered was that I wanted to play, and there was no place where I could play. Sometimes, no time either—that's it—time and place—work all day and half the night, or all night and half the day. There were days I didn't even have a room. Slept in subways and when cops saw my case, they raised their eyebrows wiselike and said, 'Ah, a virtuoso!' Jesus! those were terrible days."

The night had deepened, and through the windows I could no longer see the other walls beyond the inner court where the grass was withered. And in the lighted room, Manuel seemed older.

"But now, you can . . ." I started to say.

"What's the use?" he interrupted me. "Besides, look at my hands!"

They were old and withered like dead grass. It was true. They did not look like a violinist's hands.

"Now, do you see?" he asked. And I recalled faintly his letters from California—working in the fields, chopping wood, hoboing—Fresno, Sacramento, Alaska, Chicago, New York.

I wanted another drink. My throat was dry again, but instead I said, "I think I'd better be going."

Manuel said nothing. He just looked at me and followed me to the door.

"Goodbye," I said.

"Come again sometime, Ben, before I start in this business of dying for our country." He spoke wearily and seemed very tired indeed.

He took out a cigarette case from his shirt pocket, and again I saw his hands—these had aged, unlike his face, they had died long ago. He held out the packet to me.

"Say," he drawled in his beery breath, and looked at Helen.

"No, thanks," I answered, looking at the girl playing cards on the bed, "I don't smoke."

Back in my own room, I felt as if someone I knew had died, and in the darkness I was missing him. I walked toward the window. Overhead, somewhere in the skies above the city, came the drone of an airplane. The white girl in the other room, the one I saw on my first night in New York, was on her knees by her bed. She was praying. There was no image of a saint on the wall, only a picture of the Waldorf-Astoria in color print.

# THE HURT MEN

*The first time I heard Ambo's name mentioned was during a poker* game in our apartment at the Chalfonte Gardens in Washington, D.C., on the eve of my departure for Miami. It was a hot, sticky summer night. All day a dark mist hung over the Potomac, shutting off the sun, but never quite fulfilling what looked like a promise of rain. Dusk fell early and there was no breath of wind anywhere. In the nearby park, the trees stood postcard still. Only the men and the women lying on the grass showed life, yet the movements they made, even the slim and the supple of form, were slow, lazy, almost unwilling.

I had been home all evening packing my things. And just as I had finally succeeded in compressing a stubborn bulge in the large suitcase, there was a loud knock on the door.

They would come at a time like this, I said to myself for I knew who they were; but somehow I was glad that they had come. Then I could say to them, goodbye, friends, and we would joke and say a lot of things, meaningless perhaps, but somehow, there would not be too much heaviness around the heart any more.

I went to the door and opened it, and the boys walked in, with Teroy ahead of them.

"Poker, poker!" he cried, throwing his jacket on the nearest chair. One year at Harvard had not made clear his manner of saying things. The nasal quality in his voice was due to a chronic sinus trouble that irritated him especially in summer.

He had a half-smile and very wet lips, and, yes, he was charming in a quiet elemental way.

Mike turned on the radio. Even in the homes of strangers he would look around for the radio, and walk toward it with a hypnotic glint in his eyes, and turn it on. We had apologized for him many a time, saying he knew not what he did. He was a radio specialist, but had secret ambitions in the theater.

"He can play the role of dying man to perfection," we would say. For Mike was sickly-looking. His skin had a deathly pallor, and when we would mention this to him, he would say, "But this pallor is only skin deep." Tonight he looked frankly unhealthy; his hair was long and dry; and the pimples on his face were in a triumphant bloom.

Leo sat in a chair smiling his indeterminate smile—a satanic leer or a cherubic grin, depending on how much you liked him or how little—and saying, "All the time. All the time," a sort of meaningless refrain, but often handy camouflage to a multitude of things. Also a Harvard man, but actually graduated from the University of Chicago, he was beloved of the women. He was tall and he had dancing feet; and he knew Whitman, every grassy leaf of him. "I dote on myself," he says sometimes, quoting Whitman, "There is that lot of me and all so luscious." To which we said, he was only over-ripe.

There was another boy with them tonight, whom I had not met before, and Teroy said, "Ben, this is Val. Valentin Lopez. From Iloilo, is that right?"

"From the Philippines," Val answered.

"That's better," Teroy acknowledged the sentiment with a courtly bow, and added, "but lately from New York pretending to study."

"That's the best we can do," I said. "And now, feel at home, Val. But since when have you fallen into bad company?" I looked at Teroy who was walking toward the refrigerator.

Val laughed. It was young healthy laughter. Crinkles formed around his eyes. He had a light complexion, lighter than any of ours, and his hands, and arms as he rolled his sleeves, were plump and soft like a girl's.

"I understand you went to Columbia," he said.

"1942," I answered.

"Funny, I missed you," he said, "I was there, too."

I told him where I stayed, and he said, "But we were neighbors. That's on Claremont Avenue, isn't it? What crowd did you . . ."

"No crowd," I said, "I just went with Villa."

"Ah, the poet," said Val, "that explains everything. You were out of the world."

And very much like a scream from that other world came Teroy's disgusted oath as he came into the living room, wiping his mouth, and holding forth a glass of milk.

"What's this?" he asked. "Sour milk!"

"That's buttermilk," I said, "that's what it says on the cover of the bottle. I thought they taught you how to read in Harvard."

"Buttermilk?" said Leo. "Is Doc here?"

Doc and I shared the apartment. It was spacious and expensive and very useful. Among us all nobody drank buttermilk except Doc.

Mike turned off the radio, cutting into Bing Crosby crooning an Irish lullaby. "I get sleepy every time I hear that," he said.

Teroy went into the bedroom, and we heard him telling Doc, "Time to get up, my little butterfly, here's buttermilk for thee." This he repeated a few times and came out, saying, "He won't wake up. Maybe he's drugged. You never can tell about doctors, you know, even those who come from Johns Hopkins." Then he went to the kitchen and threw the buttermilk into the sink.

Mike was fixing the card table, wiping the dust off the top and arranging seats around it.

"I have a new deck," said Leo, fishing it out of his pocket and laying it on the table. Then he went to the porch. "It's cooler out here," he said after a while.

I went to lock my suitcase and put it out of the way. Val said, "Let me help you."

"Thanks," I said.

"Where are you going anyway?" Teroy asked.

"Miami," I answered.

"You're nuts," said Teroy, "who ever goes to Miami in summer?"

"I'm going," I insisted, "and I don't want to play poker. The Southern Limited leaves at 8 o'clock in the morning."

"You won't be late," Teroy said. "We'll stop before eight in the morning. I'll drive you in my car."

"You can drive half-asleep, I suppose."

"We'll take a chance."

Leo came out of the porch, saying, "Did you see the man lying there on the grass in the park? In summer it isn't easy to tell how many of them have homes and how many are homeless."

"All the time . . . all the time . . . nuts!" Mike mimicked, shuffling the cards impatiently.

"I'm sorry," said Leo, taking a seat. For Leo shouldn't have talked of home or of the homeless.

"Deal me in," said a sleepy voice from the bedroom. The boys laughed. They had taken off their jackets, now they were removing their ties, taking seats around the table, placing bills and silver in front of them.

"Do you have an extra pair of slippers?" Teroy asked, removing his shoes.

"Do you want pajamas, too?" I asked, throwing him a pair of slippers.

"Going to Miami in the summer," he mumbled, "I'm sure you're nuts."

Then Doc appeared at the doorway, looking more frail and delicate in silk pajamas. His eyes, naturally half-shut as though unable to stand so much light, were practically closed. "Deal me in," he repeated as he walked toward the bathroom.

When he came back, he had a fat bottle half full of coins and folded paper bills.

"Where do you keep this thing?" Mike asked, holding the bottle in his hand.

"In the refrigerator," said Doc, taking a seat.

"Really?" said Teroy, "your frozen assets, I suppose."

"I haven't met the gentleman," said Doc, smiling at Val.

"He's no gentleman," said Teroy, "But who is?" And he introduced them with the inane remark that Val better keep his girls away from Doc, Doc having specialized in *infernal* medicine.

"All the time . . . all the time," said Leo, but he evidently liked the pun.

I had changed my mind and had taken a seat myself. "When I lose this," I said, indicating the money I had placed in front of me, "I'll quit. I don't want to starve in Miami."

"You will starve in Miami," said Val. "The Army and Navy's there."

"Dealer's choice," said Mike, "table stakes."

"Miami in summer," sighed Teroy, "as if Washington isn't bad enough."

The rain promised early in the day hadn't come. Now the dark of the mist over the Potomac was one with the night, without stars, without wind. The city was trying to sleep perhaps like the figures on the grass, indolent, dissatisfied. Now and then through the night came a roar of a caged lion in the Zoo—a panting roar, far from indolent, but dissatisfied, almost human in its discontent.

"The lion wants to play. 'Deal me in . . . deal me in . . .' he's saying," said Mike.

"It's a she," said Leo.

"How do you know?" asked Doc.

"Leave it to Leo," said Teroy smiling his half-smile. "He knows."

"All the time . . . all the time . . ." said Leo.

And much of the time I was winning. It looked as though I would have to sit up playing till morning. But maybe, I said to myself, I would be able to sleep all day on the train.

It was past three in the morning. Now a soft wind straying from the river, passing over the trees on Rock Creek Park, came through the open porch, and we sighed with relief. But the wind was quickly gone, leaving us warm and restless. Mike would whistle softly for the wind, a low wailing whistle like an invitation, in the manner of provincial lads out in the Philippines, flying their kites on clear summer days.

It was Mike's deal. "Draw," he said. In the night an extra pimple had blossomed on his nose.

Val opened. He was smooth, cool and unflustered, like a student prince who remains deliberately untouched after a night's orgy. His feminine hands held the cards as in a caress. "Five dollars," he said, "for my lovely hand."

"The current price even for the loveliest," said Leo, "is only three and a half. But like a gentleman, I'm in."

We all got in, Doc putting in his five dollars dubiously. "Fools rush in," he said, "only once."

"This is going to be good," said Teroy, as he dipped a stopper into a little bottle, bent his head way back, and dropped the liquid slowly, two drops into each nostril.

I watched him fascinated. There was nothing to worry about. I held a natural flush, ace, jack high.

"The only trouble," Teroy said, choking a little. "It gets into the throat."

"I know a better way for that throat," I volunteered.

"No cards," said Val. And we all looked at him.

"*Puñeta,*" Teroy exclaimed, lapsing into what he called his father's favorite swear word.

How often in the same apartment had he talked about his father, with all the admiration and respect and love a grateful son could hold for a father whom the world was now reviling. "They call my father a Japanese puppet," he said without apparent bitterness, "but what has he done, what has he said against this great country that now vents its anger upon the father and the son?" "History will take care of him," I said. But Leo was not so sure. "By the time history is ready with its judgment, where would we be?" he said. Leo's father was the President of a university. In the sack of Manila, his father and mother and his brother and sisters were massacred after their house had been burned to the ground. It was winter still when he got the news, and for some time, he was absent from the crowd. "What we need is a prophet," said Mike, "not historians. Historians are fallible." Mike's wife was well known for her charities before the war. She was pretty as a doll. Mike's first news of home was that his wife had divorced him during the Japanese occupation. And all Mike said, "I wonder what happened to my son." Doc hadn't said a thing. He had not spoken much since he received the news of his wife's death, also in the sack of Manila. In our bedroom was a picture of her, frail and little with dark, trusting eyes. But now Doc spoke saying, "Even a prophet will not do. History will paralyze him."

Now in this crowd it was only Val whom I did not know well and love like a brother. He might be different. He looked so untouched. But who can tell? Behind that princely mien, he might also be like one of us, a hurt man. Most of us boys kept a smarting hurt beneath our brown skin, a personal tragedy of the war zealously kept, as we walked the streets of the big cities of America, seemingly gay, and uncaring; eager for friendship, grateful for the kind word, the understanding look, the touch of love.

Teroy took two cards and started sniffing.

"Give me three," said the doctor. Then he looked at his cards and threw them down. "Who wants buttermilk?" he asked, and left the table.

"Two cards," said Leo, shuffling his cards feverishly, as if engaged in his own private game.

When Mike turned to me, I shook my head. "No cards," I said, stifling a yawn.

They all looked at me, but Val was smiling. Leo had not yet seen his cards. He was smoking furiously.

"I'll take three," said Mike, helping himself. His face seemed all lit up with very ripe pimples.

Doc had returned with a glass of buttermilk and now watched us as though amused at the sight we presented. While the others were peering at their cards, Val and I were eyeing each other. The most you can have, I was telling him in my thoughts, is a natural straight, ace high perhaps. I wouldn't care. Or perhaps you're bluffing, which is just too bad. I'll have to teach you how to be honest next time. But maybe you have a flush, my good looking student prince, king high at most. No. This is my game, Val. Teroy and Mike and Doc are out. If Leo got a straight, he will go through an excruciating pain of to be or not to be. How nice. I'll sleep all day on the train. It will be air-conditioned just right. The porter will give me a pillow. I'll tip him handsomely. I would be able to afford it after this game.

"Why didn't I see you in Columbia?" Val said, breaking into my thoughts.

"Opener, please," said Leo in a rasping, overanxious voice. Poor friend, you have a straight!

Val was counting the money before him with obvious meticulous care. The lion at the Zoo must have fallen asleep. Everything was quiet now, except for the sound of a car, skidding around the bend at Argonne Place.

"Fifty," said Val, putting the money into the pot.

Doc drank his milk. Leo's lips trembled. He looked at the money in front of him and fingered the paper bills which stuck to his wet fingers. He wiped his brow with a perfumed handkerchief and I wanted to crack a joke about the handkerchief, but he looked so funereal. Then he started to light another cigarette.

"Damn it," he said as he burned his fingers.

Teroy blew his nose. The air was surcharged with something like pain. Self-inflicted. Why must we do this to one another? I started to make a recount of the pimples on Mike's fertile face.

"Call," said Leo, counting fifty dollars into the pot. "Last money," and I thought he said lost money. He had gathered the few dollars left and placed them in his pocket.

"Soon it will be dawn," he said, as if announcing some person's hanging. Now that he had finally made his decision, he was smiling again his peculiarly intriguing but happy smile.

Teroy's turn. Now his lips were contorted in deep thought, the half-smile completely obliterated. He bent over and dropped some more liquid into his nostrils. He started to count his money, but he stopped. "You got two cards," he said softly, turning to Leo as though accusing him.

"All the time, all the time," Leo answered.

"Pass," Teroy said, all the misery in his face gradually lifting.

"I'm going to bed," said Doc, and turning to Teroy, added, "You can sleep on that couch."

I was calm. I was wide awake. There was no hesitancy in my manner, no sluggishness.

"Call," I said, almost sweetly, "and fifty more." I was so engrossed in my private battle with Val, I had forgotten Mike. He looked sick when I turned to him. Then he began to hum "El Rancho Grande" softly, grimly, looking at his cards as though the melody were printed there.

"That's his swan song," Teroy said, "I shudder to hear it."

Mike threw his cards away. "I'm out," he said, and then he smiled at me. "Out, out brief candle."

Val had taken up the tune. "A beautiful swan song," he said, an amused smile brightening his face, "I wish I had one."

"Won't a dirge do?" I mocked, eager for conflict.

Val counted fifty dollars. "That's a lot of money," he said, "anywhere you come from," and still smiling, added, "but there's some more left here."

Pushing the undetermined amount into the pot, he said, "There's the fifty, plus this, if you don't mind too much."

"Aren't you a little reckless?" I asked, smiling at him as sweetly as I could.

It was then that Val mentioned Ambo's name. "You see, Ben," he said, "I have been watching you throughout the game. You are all right. Have you heard of Ambo? You should meet Ambo." Then he counted the money in excess of the fifty.

"Thirty-seven and seventy-five cents," he announced.

"And the cents, too?" I asked solicitously, "Truly, you are reckless."

"I bet my last money," Leo said, wishing to be remembered. Val was saying, "I like you, Ben. You should meet Ambo. It's surprising that you haven't met him yet . . . oh, no it isn't. But he lives in Washington. Out in New York we know him very well. Haven't you even heard of Ambo? There's only one Ambo in the entire Atlantic seaboard."

"Thirty-seven, seventy-five," I said, pushing the money into the pot. "What have you got?"

The other boys seemed more nervous than either Val or I.

Val put his hands on his cards and spoke softly, almost gently. "When are you getting back from Miami? You should meet Ambo immediately. I can arrange a meeting. Swell guy.

You'd love playing with him." Then, as though it were only an afterthought, something incidental to a more momentous thing like meeting Ambo, he spread his cards on the table.

"Flush," he said, "Ace, jack high."

"What?" I shouted, losing my sweetness and all my composure.

"Damn it!" said Leo throwing his cards into the discarded pile.

I laid my cards on the table.

"Ace, jack high," I said, showing the diamond flush.

"Good Lord," Val exclaimed.

"I have a nine," I said in the vaguest of whispers.

"Your nine wins," said Val, "I have only a five."

Inside me there was a sickening emptiness, like sudden hunger. Val pushed the money towards me graciously.

"Ben," he said, "you should meet Ambo."

All the way down to Miami on the Southern Limited, I kept thinking of Ambo. Who was he? And why should I meet him?

## MANILA HOUSE

*A gradually demobilizing navy hastened my return to Washington.*
Besides, I was going back to school, this time to Cambridge
where Teroy and Leo had studied. In Miami I was privileged
to witness the miracle of the English language. A thousand
Chinese sailors and some hundred Russian seamen and
officers landed in Miami off Biscayne Bay without any knowledge of English, a number of the Chinese even illiterates in
their own tongues. In a few weeks, they were sailing their
ships, giving and taking commands in Basic English with
American seamen and officers. Behind this miracle of the written and the spoken word was a staff of Harvard professors
under whom I was going to work in the fall.

The boys were sincerely glad to see me back. A return after
an absence often affords the pleasant discovery that one's company could be missed. Not the obvious sentimental word of
welcome or the eloquent sigh, but the bantering, subtle ways
these boys could say they missed you, without actually saying
the words.

"I suppose we should be glad to see you back as your presence here gives us a chance to get our money back."

"Gamblers!" I said.

"How's Miami Beach? How are the girls?"

"Miami Beach is still there. As usual the ocean has been par-
titioned into private beach fronts and green and red cabanas;
and as for the second question, Doc, are you talking as a man
of science interested in the human anatomy?"

"Come, come," said Leo, "tell us, Are the girls there the
same as here they be?"

"Your language interests me more than your question."

And I told them about the mosquitoes, how they tore at you in hordes and bit you in the most sacred places without shame, without a recoil in the springs of their consciences.

"What language!" said Teroy, "Basic English should do you a lot of good. But I don't know how you'd fare in Cambridge. What will interest you there? Your sense of wonder is practically nil, how could you delight in the magical achievement of the glass flowers at Peabody Museum? The lectures on and off the Yard will definitely be far over your head. And lacking in any sense of history, you will be blind to the historic spots in Cambridge and Greater Boston. They will be nothing to you but plaques and monuments, and half hidden promontories of stone and grass, open to both wind and sun. And you will be deaf to the whisper of the ages . . . and you can't play poker there."

"What language, he says!" I taunted Teroy, "Did you hear that speech?"

"Really, Ben," Teroy said. "You would be happier here with us. There's nothing in Cambridge except dead heroes and half-dead intellectuals mumbling Homer, and the oldest women you ever saw, mumbling . . . just mumbling."

"Ben, you fill my heart with commiseration," Teroy spoke again.

"He means pity," Doc interrupted.

"You fill my heart with commiseration," Teroy repeated; "I cannot imagine how unhappy you would be in the hub of so much culture. You will be a lost soul. You will be bruised. You will be lacerated, and you make such a convenient victim, what with your intellectual nakedness."

"This is enjoyable," I said, for, really, I was enjoying it. I knew that these boys were sort of envious because they were not going back to the university with me.

"And one day," Teroy seemed ludicrously affected by the sentiment of what he was to say, "before the term is over and you decide to end your misery into the depths no less of historic Charles River, don't say I didn't warn you," and he bowed himself out into the bathroom.

I turned to Doc, "I see there's no letter for me," I said. When

we talked of letters we didn't mean letters from Jim or Mary of
New York or from Al in Pennsylvania, and Diony from San
Francisco. We meant letters from home.

Doc shook his head. "But Teroy got one it seems. I don't
know what, but he's thinking of selling his car to send something, he says, to his mother."

Then Teroy came out of the bathroom, saying. "In all
seriousness, Ben, I think you are a lucky dog. But tell me, how
strong are your convictions? Or do you have any sort of faith
at all? I don't mean whether you go to church or not. I don't
mean the physical gestures and the carryover of childhood
piety. I mean this," pointing to his heart, "what it believes is
the true word, the one faith."

"I don't know," I answered suddenly unsure of myself and
wishing I had a letter from home, then I would have been less
uncertain.

"Or don't you have any sort of faith at all"? Teroy asked. We
looked at one another. We were not the gay boys any more
that instant, who filled the apartment with the sound of our
young voices, our laughter, and our brave words. We had
such moments.

I remembered how during the first days of the war when a
terrible anxiety gripped our hearts about the fate of those we
loved in the Philippines, we walked alone and found ourselves
kneeling in deserted corners of many a church, whispering to
God. How we sat by ourselves in the park, by the riverside,
talking to God. And as the years rolled on, a terrible dullness
in the heart, and a dryness on the lips that prayed no more,
that asked for nothing now, that cared for less. And then an
awakening of hope as we watched the mighty strength of
America, moving at last, toward victory.

"You would be better off without faith," Teroy was saying,
"then there's nothing those old men of Harvard could destroy;
for when they do destroy, they do it in the purest of prose
imaginable."

"All the time . . . all the time . . ." said Leo, shaking his
head in laughter, and somehow we were young again, truly
and magnificently young.

"What about the dark girl from Rumania you mentioned in your letter, Ben?" Doc asked.

"Have I told you she's a well-known painter in Europe?"

"A painter?" the doctor gasped, "Did she make you?"

"I was only too willing," I said.

"Ben, you amaze me," said Val, "you should see Ambo."

"Now, who the hell is this Ambo?"

"That's why I want you to meet him," said Val, who, I understood, stayed more often now in Washington than in New York.

"Let's invite him to the apartment then," I said.

"He won't accept the invitation," Val answered. "Ambo is a proud little man. He thinks we are snobs."

"He must be all right," said Teroy, "I'd want to meet him. Anybody who'd come to one of us and says, 'you're a snob,' must be all right. That's calling a spade a spade."

"I wouldn't say that," said Mike.

"Now let us be honest to ourselves," Teroy replied.

"All the time . . . all the time . . ." said Leo. "Now tell us about Ambo."

Val said, "Ambo is a little elderly Filipino who is now engaged in the dangerous work of tinkering with explosives. He says he isn't doing it for patriotism, but for the money. He had been everything else before the war. The boys look up to him. I have heard that during the depression years he had a whole household of Filipinos, feeding on everything he could give them, and he was tireless. Now those whom he saw through those years will fight for him, will die for him. He is well loved by the Filipino community. If he had only been educated, he would have been an articulate leader of our countrymen in this country. But even as he is, they respect him, because he has something they haven't got, most of them, and that's integrity. He should really be one of us, if we were not the snobs he calls us. Incidentally, he knows very little Tagalog, but it is better than his English. His Visayan is classic. I should know. But though his English is not exactly flawless, his poker is."

"You mean." I said, "that he has a sense of smell?"

"That's it. That's it." Val cried. "That's what he got. That's what you got, too. That's why I would want to see you play."

"Sense of smell!" Teroy sniffed. "Don't be ridiculous. Give me a good hand and you can have all the sense of smell in the world."

"I don't really mean sense of smell, Teroy," Val explained, a little embarrassed, because Teroy, with his sinus trouble, had not much of a sense of smell.

"Ambo's a professional gambler then," I said. "In which case I would not want to play with him. I'm not such a good player myself. If I had been winning of late, it was the sort of luck the superstitious often ascribe to men of goodwill and merry Christmas hearts. Or in Doc's inimitable grammar, 'Now I'm lucky, now I don't!' "

"Oh, no, Ambo is not a professional gambler, I have never seen a more nervous player in my life. And talk of poker face, this man has all sorts of facial expressions for all kinds of hands. You'd pity him, the first time you play him, till you see the money piling up in front of him."

"We have to see this man," said Teroy, more eager than I.

So we set out to see Ambo. It was said that he frequented the Manila House on K and 4th Streets. It's a two-story building painted white. It's on the left from the Washington Circle, in the periphery of the colored section of the Capital. That's where Filipinos lived mainly, in sections of the city that were not yet truly colored sections, but were less white. Through the years the Filipino communities served as happy painless transition. That's what happened on 18th Street Northwest, in and around the twenty-third hundred block between Belmont and California Streets; that's what happened on 4th and F, and that's what was happening around Manila House.

They served the finest Filipino dishes there. The dining room was clean and curtained windows looked out into a garden, weedy and wild except for ripe tomatoes in summer and gigantic squash, and eggplants, and bitter melons hanging on the vine. The tables and the dishes were always clean, as were the American waitresses whom the boys sometimes ran away with and made their wives after a hurried marriage ceremony in a little town of Maryland. Sometimes there was no ceremony at all.

There were a few boys whom we had seen before, eating at some of the tables. They were mostly taxi drivers whose taxis we saw parked under the trees on K Street. There were a couple of Pullman boys, stopping over for the night in Washington. Val knew them well. In the adjoining room there was an old piano and Teroy had started playing Schubert's "Serenade." "I play this piece better than my sister does," he said, "and she went to the Conservatory."

On the newly-papered walls were the framed pictures of Rizal, Quezon, and Osmeña. In another corner of the room above the coat hangers were the American and Filipino flags, with the red and white and blue quite faded, and the lustre of the sun and the stars dimmed by the years and dust.

We were going to have dinner. A table for six was set for us near the curtained window to the rear. Val went to the kitchen and talked to the cook. It was a small kitchen. The huge refrigerator took much of the space. A fat man with dirty teeth was eating with his hands near the door, and he talked and laughed as he ate and the rice grains and particles of meat dropped all around him. Val stood by the door smiling his orders to the cook who kept nodding his head. The waitress edged sidewise through the door, her all sufficient breasts pushing against Val's back, but Val kept smiling his instructions.

Leo was watching a group playing knock rummy near the door facing K Street. Mike and Doc were wandering around restlessly, pausing now and then before some yellowed picture on the walls and above the fireplace. Teroy was still at the piano going through the first bars of a Chopin "Polonaise" as though he was groping in the dark. He would falter and miss his way, then retrace his steps, more uncertain than before, give up altogether and try another piece, and still another, without quite getting a start in some instances.

"I'm what you'd call," he said, "a *chopsuey* artist."

"You're not even a piano tuner," said Mike, "why don't you think of these boys' sensibilities?"

The boys smiled at us because we were laughing. They knew we were making fun of Teroy and they enjoyed it, too. Some of them were loudmouthed and talked of the usual things; their conquest of fair ladies, real or imagined, and fabulous bets won and lost on the gaming tables in Chinatown. Many of them had been in uniform, but had been honorably discharged on account of age. When they turned to us to ask a question, it would usually begin with, "Is it true . . ." Then we would tell them. They would shout at one another in argument, nearly come to blows, say on such a technical question as citizenship, which, to them, was not technical but sentimental. They would make us judge and sometimes we ourselves were a little uncertain of our opinion. Except Teroy, Teroy was cocksure about certain things. He had a good appetite, too.

It was a feast laid before us, and as we sat down, we remembered the nice thing to do; each one of us turned in every direction where the boys were talking and playing and said with our eyes and our lips: "Come, let's eat." And the boys responded with the usual, "Thanks, we have already eaten," or "Thank you, I've already given my order." From a few came just a nod to show that the invitation was well taken.

My friends had varied eating habits: Doc was a good cook himself. At the apartment he turned out the most delicious crabmeat omelette I have ever tasted; and such delicious pancakes, about which I would ask what the recipe was and he would say, "It's a prayer." But he ate scantily like a bird, a little bird. "Superb," he said, after tasting two or three of the delicacies laid before us.

Teroy had no time for anything else, not for talk nor anything, during the first five or ten minutes, at least. He gobbled the food like a hungry genius.

Leo didn't want anything with vinegar, not the faintest sour flavor. Now he kept asking, "Which of this ain't tainted?" Mike had a flat appetite as usual. "The eyes are willing," he said, "but only the eyes."

Val ate like a prince, and the waitress hovered about him, solicitous, ministering. Evidently, she knew him, for among us, he came here oftenest.

Mike said something to a boy across the table, and the boy said something and they both laughed. Others joined in the laughter and soon there were many boys in the room, and everybody was talking at the same time. Some of the boys were dressed in garbardine suits, others in dilapidated silk that must have seen years of service. Leo and Teroy wore light tweeds. Val was becoming in his white palm beach. Most of the other boys wore nothing but shirts opened at the throat, and baggy trousers.

One boy said, "How about that citizenship bill, Doc?" He didn't mean Doc. He meant any one of us. Leo gave an exposition on the possibility of its passing; the probable source of opposition, its nature, and the bright hopes of surmounting it, Leo was succinct; he was scholarly.

Then there was another question. "Are you sure they're gonna give us our independence; what's that 'as soon as feasible' meant?"

Teroy explained it so well I found myself listening to him intently though I had heard it explained a number of times.

"Ah, big shots!" said a voice from the rear. Evidently, the man had just come in.

"But you see," said Teroy, "the economics of a country, especially a country like ours, ruined, devastated, cut into helpless bits, is inextricably linked with, and naturally affects, the soundness of its political independence."

That was too much. Leo said simply, "Economic distress leads to unrest."

"You mean we're gonna have a civil war down there?" asked an old looking boy with a dirty shirt.

"Not a civil war maybe," Leo answered, "but great unrest. The peasants of the Philippines are up in arms. They will not return to the farm under the same old conditions of serfdom that they and their fathers knew and their fathers before them."

"But the bloodshed!" said the Prince. "And I understand, some of the peasants' demands are downright unreasonable."

Leo made circular motions with his hands. "The wheel has turned," he said. "The peasants are demanding, you say. The landlords before the war never demanded; they took."

"What they took was their own," said the Prince without anger, without heat.

"Yes, their own, after years and years of cumulative grabbing," said Leo.

"Would you say the Church is also a grabbing landlord?" Mike asked.

"A subtle one." said Leo, "and untouchable. You cannot drive sticks into his eyes and a knife into his bloated abdomen, nor blow his brains out. No. And he has come into his huge possessions not through hands stretched out to grab, but through hands stretched out in supplication, in prayer, in well meaning concern over the soul. And as it happened, our landed ancestors had great concern over their souls and were willing to turn over their property to the church to help contribute to the upkeep of their souls in the hereafter."

"You have heard of the lawlessness now pervading the land, haven't you?" Val persisted, yet seemed unwilling to say something more. Then he added, as if it were not relevant to the matter at all, "My father was kind to his tenants. He was kind to everybody. He had a big family, my father; and his tenants were not the least of them all. And they loved him. They were happy under him. As a child, I sat on their muddy knees, listening to their crude, man songs. They carried me on their strong shoulders across wild streams, through dangerous woods. I spent the night in their huts and they loved me. I loved them too. We were a great family. Wherever I went among my father's lands I saw no unrest, but a placid contentment. I went to school with our tenants' sons. The day I left home for America, the tenants saw me off with tears in their eyes. In the years that followed, when I thought of father and mother, I thought of them too."

Nobody spoke. The waitress was looking at him as though she could swallow him whole. He was so good looking, so much like a prince among men.

"And one day, not very long ago," Val continued, "Father was talking to them out in the fields. There were some strange men among them, and they were demanding . . . yes, Leo, that's it, they were demanding, and Father was listening to them; then they rushed upon him, even those that loved him, those who wept at my departure, they rushed upon him, leaving him dead upon the untilled fields."

Val was not crying. "That's just what I meant," he said to Leo, smiling sadly, and adding, "it may be the wheel has turned, but the rim is sodden with men's flesh, and the spokes are splattered with blood. It isn't a pretty picture."

"I'm sorry," said Leo.

And the boys started walking about, saying nothing. The waitress wiped her eyes with her apron and started taking away the plates.

Leo turned to me and said, "I wish my father had died in an open field. It would have been a cleaner death . . . but not . . . I'm being sentimental."

"Boys," said Teroy, in an unusually loud voice, "will you have dessert?"

# A PECULIAR RUSTLING

*Dessert consisted of overripe bananas, sweet to the taste, and* weak coffee, served complete with sugar and cream. Yet we lingered over our cups. It was still daylight when we came. Now the dusk had come in a burst of glaring lights. Now I remembered my first sight of the Capitol in a flood of light, subdued and symbolic, after many years of darkness; the quiet inspiring beauty of the Lincoln monument on an evening of rain, with the rain seeming to fall heaviest under the street lamps; how I stood there speechless and awed by the magnificence of the man, translated into marble, by the magnificence of his words, carved into stone: FOURSCORE AND SEVEN YEARS AGO, and glimpses of my childhood came rushing back: my voice rising above the din and clatter of a Tondo evening as I recited Lincoln's Gettysburg Address. These very words, hard in my memory as the stone into which they had been carved . . . how many of these boys had made the pilgrimage, how many of them had taken time out of their many empty hours to look into the sad eyes of Lincoln, to read the words again in silence? What have these landmarks of history meant to them, Lincoln's poverty and his heart of gold, and his deep terrible sadness? Meaningless . . . meaningless. In spring and summertime, they have walked in the parks, and have posed for pictures, little brown man in an expensive suit, arm around the waist of a smiling—often a little taller—American girl, the Lincoln Memorial for background or the dome of the Capitol rising above the trees, or the Washington monument tall

58

against the skies, to mark the place as on a day in spring, the important thing through the ages being the brown man's arm around the white girl's waist.

A few boys were arriving with their girl friends, clean looking and respectable; a number of them, I was sure, married couples. These American girls ate Philippine dishes with relish, held their spoons in the right hands, with the fork in the left as a pusher only, the chief means of conveyance to the mouth, being the spoon. How Filipino! How entrancing are native ways performed with grace and love by those not to the manner born! Now and then we would hear these ladies uttering Filipino expressions with a naturalness that was engaging! *Sigue na,* with an inviting twinkle in the eyes; *Ikaw naman,* with a reproaching wave of the hand; *Ang sarap,* with a satisfied smacking of the lips.

The card tables had been moved farther into another room, and the huge hall in the middle had been tidied over, folding chairs unfolded and stood against the walls. Several boys walked in with musical instruments, violins and saxophones in boxes, and guitars and mandolins in green bags.

"I forgot all about it," said Val, "there's going to be a dance tonight. Of course, you don't mind."

That didn't need an answer. Val called the waitress and she came to him, beaming as much as she could beam in an apron and the smell of onions and garlic upon her.

"How much is it?" asked Val. We all dipped our hands in our pockets for our share of the bill.

The waitress smiled. She bent over and whispered something to Val.

"What's this?" we asked.

"Gentlemen," Val announced, "we have just had a free dinner."

"How's that?"

"Ambo paid for it," said Val, "I'll go and fetch him."

He went to the other room where the boys were playing, and he came back with the brother of Rizal. Or so he looked, this man called Ambo. He seemed as old as Rizal himself in his pictures. But remove the coat and the hard collar; part the lips in a shy smile; carve away deep lines around the mouth and under the eyes, daub the edges of his collar with the stain of hard work or simple carelessness; and instead of a black tie, a green tie threadbare with many years of fingering. And that was Ambo as he stood there like a happy peasant, one among us now, or if he had been Rizal himself, this one was without innocence, this one was weary of martyrdom and grown tired with songs and love of country.

We shook hands with him. His hand was heavy and tightly veined, calloused and black at the finger tips.

"So this is Ambo," I said, wondering whether the others had remarked the similarity between him and the hero of our country. Apparently nobody did. Otherwise they would have expressed it or Val could have said it in his description of the man.

"You didn't have to pay for our dinner," said Teroy. "That was a lot to pay. Besides . . ."

"Dat's awright . . . dat's awright," Ambo said in his own brand of English, waving his hand, "dat's nebber mind atoll."

It seemed, he hadn't paid for our dinner really. He was practically the manager of the Club. When the proprietor and the cook ran out of cash, Ambo was always ready to help them out.

We were profuse with thanks and understanding.

"When did you get here anyhow?" Val asked.

"In the middle of speeches," Ambo said. Then he turned to Val. "Noble man, his father like god."

"Ambo knew my father," Val explained.

"You speak Visayan?" Ambo asked the crowd.

We said yes almost to a man.

"How happy!" said Ambo, and those were practically the last words in English he ever uttered when alone with us telling a story.

"Now," he said, eager to talk in the dialect, and very much at ease, "how long have you been in America? This war has hurt many people."

"Yes, yes," said Val, "but we didn't come here to talk about it. I brought my friends here to have some sort of recreation."

"In a few hours there will be a dance," said Ambo. "The girls will steal your hearts. They all love Val because he is so beautiful. But I don't want Val to get into trouble. The first time he was here, I told him that every time he danced with a girl, he should look at me. If I nodded, that meant that the girl was nobody's girl and he could go ahead; if I looked away, that meant, go slow, she's somebody's girl, but the guy is overseas; but if I started scratching my nose, he should stay away, the boy friend's around."

We were laughing before he was through with his explanation. "Will you do that for all of us tonight?" Mike said.

Ambo swayed as he laughed, "You better be good boys." he said. "If you all turn out to be like Val, I shall have a headache. Did you know that when he liked the girl, it didn't matter whether I kept scratching my nose till it bled, he went ahead just the same . . . and well . . . I don't want any trouble for my friends."

"There will be no trouble," said Val. "We're not in a dancing mood tonight."

"Pray, may I ask," said Leo, "what is the mood we are in tonight?"

Val ignored him. "We want a little mental exercise. Poker maybe."

"Ah," said Ambo, twinkling all over.

"Val isn't going to play," said Leo. "He'll do some nose scratching for me tonight."

As it turned out, the boys preferred dancing to poker. I sat opposite Ambo at a round table covered with an Army blanket. There were three other boys. They had much money and they were good. But there was something in the atmosphere that disgusted me, the suffocating air perhaps, or the stench of something foul out of the darkness. Or perhaps it was because I didn't know the players. They were all strangers to me, not excluding Ambo. Then I had difficulty keeping myself from laughing at the way Ambo's hands trembled. Especially when he dealt—the cards went all over the table. If I had been losing, I would have been completely disgusted and left the table to dance.

My friends must have been having a wonderful time. The Filipino orchestra was good. The music was soft, nearly always, and the soloist sang with feeling:

*If I love you . . . time and again . . .*

From where I sat, I could see the orchestra at the farthest end of the dance floor. A lace curtain divided the gambling room from the dance hall. I could see the dancers. The girls seemed graceful. A number of them wore black dresses, and from that distance, they didn't look bad at all. The boys had natural grace of movement, unstudied, perfect. Once in a while I would recognize Leo's back and Val's profile.

If there was such a thing as pure poker, maybe this was it. Nobody said anything that was not connected with the game. Once I tried to start a conversation with Ambo, but he was so busy trembling and winning that he didn't hear me at all. I was beginning to wish that the boys would come over and ask me to go—anywhere, I was not winning much. Ambo was. And he looked so nervous, I'm sure he actually was, he seemed as though he would break into pieces any time. The other boys were no mean players either. But they didn't say anything. The game seemed like a matter of life and death to them. They didn't smile even when they won.

Teroy came over, saying that he was leaving with Doc and Mike. They had three girls with them whom they were taking to the Madrillon.

"Would you want us to come back for you?" he asked.

"That wouldn't be necessary," I answered. "Maybe Leo could take me in his car."

"And how are you doing?" he asked.

"Not bad," I replied.

"You don't mind," he said, taking a twenty-dollar bill from my money.

"Help yourself," I answered, "there's more where that comes from," and I pointed at the money of the other players.

Teroy laughed. Nobody else did. Ambo was eyeing me all through the game, but he didn't smile.

"Are you ready?" asked the boy on my side. He was shuffling the cards.

"Go ahead," I said.

"Good night," said Teroy.

"Be good," said Ambo.

"If you can't be good," I said, "be careful."

"I know," said Teroy, "and if I can't be careful, I'd better be."

This time everybody laughed, except the boy who was dealing.

"Ready?" he repeated.

"Shoot!" I said, a little peeved at his over-anxiety. "Nobody's stopping you."

That deal proved to be the last game.

"Draw," said the dealer, "anything can open." As he was distributing the cards, Leo and Val came.

"Teroy left with Doc and Mike," I said.

"I know," said Leo, "We're leaving too."

"What's this?" I said, looking at my hand—a pair of treys, nothing more—"the Hegira?"

"Opener," said the dealer, turning to the man on his left. The man shook his head. With trembling hands and a pale face, Ambo looked at his hand and shook his head vehemently. The other boy said no. I said, "Nothing doing."

"I open," said the dealer, as if giving out some grave announcement. "Five dollars."

Ambo's mouth twitched, and his hands trembled so much that the table shook when he placed his hands on it. "That's robbery," he cried. " 'Cause you know we got lousy hands, you open with five dollars to make us run and you get the five dollars ante."

"Rule of the game, ain't it? Nobody's keeping you. If you think so much of your dollar, come on in, the water's fine!"

"By golly!" cried Ambo, "I'm staying in, why not?" He pushed a five dollar bill into the pot.

The other two boys dropped out. One of them giggled as though he was having fun at my expense.

"I'm in," I said. Leo and Val stood behind me without a word.

"How many?" asked the dealer, smiling at Ambo who was now looking at his cards which he held in his trembling hands.

With difficulty—it was pitiful to see him trembling like that and being made fun of—he took one of his cards and laid it face down on the table. Then he discarded the four.

"Give me four cards," he said.

The boys giggled louder.

"Look," said Ambo, his eyes flashing fire, as he took four cards from the dealer, "I ain't looking at these cards." He placed the four face down on top of his one card. Then he sat back, crossing his arms on his breast.

"Three cards," I said.

I got another trey. Three of a kind!

The dealer took three cards also. He looked at his cards and smiled at us.

"Well?" said Ambo, his arms still crossed on his breast.

"Twenty only," said the dealer.

"Twenty only?" Ambo repeated. "That's bad. And I ain't looking at my cards, and I got four, remember?" A trembling hand dropped twenty dollars into the pot, and then, very slowly, another thirty more.

"Raise you thirty," he said, his gold teeth sparkling in a smile. And looking at me, he added, "It's better you're staying out of this."

Why, this was ridiculous! Ambo must be out of his head. If he thought he could bamboozle us out of the game by this foolhardy method of his, he must be crazy indeed.

"As it happens," I said, quite certain of my three of a kind, "I'm staying in." I placed fifty dollars in the pot.

Ambo looked obviously disturbed. "Some guys can't be told," he said with grave intensity.

The dealer seemed triumphant. And I was beginning to get anxious. Maybe this guy had also three of a kind. But deep inside me I felt certain that he had only two pairs. And Ambo was playing the bluffer.

"You raise thirty, okay," said the dealer, "and fifty more."

Suddenly the air was stuffy. I didn't want those two boys standing there behind me without saying a word. The music was too loud. The stench from the outside seemed heavier.

"I ain't looking at my cards, and I got four," Ambo was saying as though to impress the magnitude of his bluff upon our dull-witted heads. He counted fifty dollars and placed it in the pot.

"And one hundred more," he said, looking very much satisfied with himself in spite of his trembling hands.

Involuntarily I placed my hands against my forehead. Because all of a sudden I was angry at Ambo. The old duffer! This was no longer a question of dollars. And the fool that I was, I thought that it was my manliness that was being tested.

"Run," said Ambo, "I got you both!"

Who would believe him? He didn't even know what he had! Was he so dense as to think that we would fall for such tom-foolery?

"You don't have to dictate," the dealer said with some anger, looking hard at Ambo, "if this man wants to stay, let him stay, he got money. Besides, this is a free country, ain't it?"

"Yep," said Ambo, his mouth frothing, "more free for fools."

"All the time . . . all the time . . ." Leo's voice came from behind me.

But after I had done it, I knew I was the biggest damn fool in Washington that night.

"Here's the fifty," I said, "and the one hundred plus one hundred more."

The dealer turned pale. He tried to smile, but didn't quite make it. He fingered his money, looked at his cards, as if by a miracle of intense wishing they would change into a winning hand. And he kept doing this several times, alternately. When I looked at Ambo, he was smiling at me, and I thought he looked like my father who never knew I had finally reached America.

Now the dealer had broken into a sweat. Finally, in a whisper that was almost inaudible, he said in the dialect, "I surrender."

"Now," said Ambo, "it's time I look at my cards."

With trembling hands he gathered them to his bosom as if to honor them with his love. It seemed, suddenly he turned pale, and when he looked at me, his smile was friendly, almost sweet.

"Son of a cat!" he exclaimed, still hugging his cards. He seemed actually enjoying himself and there I was tense like a man about to be sentenced.

"Well, now?" I said, trying to infuse strength into my body with the sound of my voice. I had no legs, and my hands were limp.

"Well, now," he repeated, "of course, I run away."

His words came to me as through a daze. I did not move. I could not. The room was full of voices. In the confusion, I saw Val run to Ambo and take his cards. He looked at them once and gave them back to Ambo who mixed them up with the other cards in spite of the requests of the other boys to see what he had.

Val placed a hand on Ambo's shoulder and said, "Why don't you go with us? We'll have drinks somewhere. Ben is throwing this party, aren't you, Ben?"

"Sure," I said, "sure," trying to feel whether I still had my legs.

"Mister Ben's a good player," Ambo said.

"Did you hear that, Ben?" Val asked, "Ambo says you're good. I knew he would like you. And now shall we go?"

Ambo volunteered to drive and I sat beside him. The two boys sat with their girls in the backseat. The girl with Val had a marked Southern drawl. She was a pretty redhead named Sue and she kept calling Val, "darling." Leo's girl was tall and dark. Her teeth weren't so good. She had two names. One of them was all I could remember, it sounded like Loo.

Both girls wanted to go to a nightclub. The boys turned to Ambo for suggestion. He said most of the nightclubs in the city would soon close up, but he knew a place in the suburbs that didn't close till after two in the morning.

"Besides," Ambo said, "we got plenty gas."

It was a long ride but exhilarating. The wind carried with it the smell of the green country. There were no more lights winking in the distance; we were fast leaving the city behind us. Now was wild wood on both sides, the swish of leaves in the wind like rain. Somewhere in my country, I thought, smoke would be rising to the skies and there would be a peculiar rustling in the bamboo groves; and a young mother would be lying fast asleep beside her three daughters, dreaming dreams, unhappy dreams mostly, but brave, and not without hope.

# NIGHTCLUB

*The Nightclub stood a little withdrawn from the road. A floodlight* shone on the parking lot on the front where cars stood shoulder to shoulder in stiff intimacy. A dim lamp shone over the gate which opened to a runway studded with lights, like the green bulbs in the subways of New York. Ambo led the way, for only those familiar with this semi-darkness knew where it led. They had the surer step.

The distance was short. We had expected music, and we heard only a voice. Perhaps the master of ceremonies introducing the next number on the floor show. Perhaps the last floor show for the night.

Then a more spacious hallway roofed in green again, like a Spanish veranda. Here couples walked about hand in hand; for here the air was fresh with the wildwood and the softness of the night.

A thickset man stood by the door which led to a dark interior. A spotlight accentuated the bigness of a woman now half-singing, half-reciting a bawdy song, while she stripped gradually. I looked at her as we were ushered to our seats, not far from the dance floor, a rectangular bit of shining wood. She had false eyelashes. Maybe she wore a wig, I thought. She was no longer young, but looked like the grandmother of a dozen whores. Her voice was mannish, and she trilled her r's and her a's were broad as her hips. Now her arms were bare, and a tantalizing portion above her knees. She looked in our direction, walked towards us, then stopped half-way to remove a flimsy underthing, which she waved in front of her like a white banner flying.

Many of the customers were not looking. Perhaps they feared the worst and a spoiled evening. The girls looked amused and superior with their own secret knowledge of their lovelier lines and curves. The men remembered better sights than this tonight in a lifetime of knowing. Or maybe they must have seen something like this before; just when she wrenched off what was supposed to be the last garment, lo and behold—nothing! For she would be as well draped as when she had started the whole thing.

Yet there would be the usual clapping of hands. The motion was easy; it was kind. Or it might be sincere or hopeful: that the next number be less grim, or better still, dance music, perhaps.

The boys ordered drinks. Loo and Sue wanted theirs double straight. Not soda, please, just plain water. Val looked at Leo significantly, and he chanted, "All the time . . . all the time . . ." The boys ordered the same.

"The orchestra's mostly Filipino," I observed.

"You are a lovely people," said one of the girls.

"What? Already?" I said, smiling.

"The guy who mixes the drinks is Filipino, too. Also the cook, makes the most fantastic sandwiches. That's why I like this place," said Ambo, proud of his knowledge.

"You go to these places quite often, Ambo?"

"Oh, every so now and then."

"What are you having?"

"I'm having," Ambo said, "*Diablo Cocktail.* That's the boy's specialty. What you say, we are having that, ha?"

I hesitated. "I'd want to see it first," I said, "then when you're through and still on your feet, I might try it the next round."

I ordered rum and coca cola, only I said, "Cuba Libre." That made it more impressive, and more expensive too.

"You'd love *Diablo Cocktail,*" Ambo assured us.

The girls were eager to see it. They were also eager to dance.

"You'll have to excuse us," said Val. As he spoke, the two girls stood, and the boys pushed back their chairs.

I stood up bowing to them. Ambo had not moved from his seat, but when he saw me standing, he pushed his chair back, but it was too late, the couples had already left.

"I'm so heavy," Ambo said.

I looked around. The Filipino members of the orchestra were looking at Loo and Val; the boys acknowledged their glances, and smiles passed through the music: The glances said, Filipino? Yes. And the smiles said, Countryman, do I know you, or have we met before, or shall we meet perhaps, it's a familiar face, Countryman; this music is for you; my steps are easy, happy moving steps, because the music is from you, Countryman.

The lights were so dim, you could hardly see the men and the women sitting it out in corners, holding hands. Everybody looked so very much in love with everybody else, I wondered how much of it was truly love, how much was music, and dimness and wine.

Now we could talk in the dialect. "Well, now," I said to Ambo, "I guess we would have to be content sitting it out all night."

"Not unless you'd prefer it that way," he answered, looking around.

"We haven't got any partners."

"That isn't a problem. Unless of course, you'd really prefer sitting down like this."

"Let's wait for our drinks," I said.

When the drinks came, the two couples had already returned to their seats, a little flushed, and so beautiful the four of them in the dim lights.

The girls quaffed their drinks without changing the expressions on their faces, without a palpable quiver on the shoulder.

Ambo's cocktail looked impressive. It was in a frozen high glass, the coldness accentuated by powdered sugar clinging on the lips of the glass like driven snow, with a green leafy plant shoved into it like a fallen green branch in the middle of an icy lake.

"That's terrible," I said. "That plant will get into your nose before you get a drop of the liquid. Or is that supposed to happen?"

"Oh, no," said Ambo. "You do it like this, see, easy only," as he picked the green leafy thing and laid it on the saucer. He stirred the liquid, and sipped tentatively. "Fantastic," he said.

"Sure is," said the girls in mock humor. They had consumed their drinks and now were looking towards our waiter, trying to catch his eye.

"Aren't you dancing?" asked Leo.

"No, not now," I answered, "Ambo and I will sit it out here and exchange secrets."

The girls giggled.

It was the same old story for Ambo as well as for thousands of other Filipino boys who were poor and didn't like school a great deal. Other young men from the provinces were going to America and their letters glowed with praise for the strange big cities of America. Often they went as houseboys of American couples, and after a while, they drifted for themselves in the small and the big cities, one menial job after another. The letters for home continued to glow with the bright hopes of the future and tales of the glitter of life in the new country. In the beginning also, there was the money order for a few dollars, which in terms of pesos doubled its amount; and the poor parents had the roof of their house patched; they bought new clothing and silverware; and soon they had a little farm of their own, and the aging parents sat at their bamboo stairs weaving bright dreams of the future for their son and for themselves.

In a few cases, the letters continued to come to Mother. They still contained the money order and bright glowing hopes. But in most instances, letters became far apart, and, in the course of time, they failed to come altogether.

Meanwhile what had happened to the son? He had dropped off school entirely. At night when he tried to study among other adults, he was so tired and what the teachers did and said did not make much sense at all. It was more relaxing, sitting near a billiard table and watching the players; or standing around guys playing cards. Soon he was gambling himself;

laughing with the men when they laughed about vulgar things that now he himself knew. At this point, the letters could not be written, the lie could not be said. Better, silence . . . He would write again. But how swift the days turned into years, how quickly tomorrow became yesterday . . .

Now the drifting from one city to another. Here would be new faces. Here would be a new lease of life. But it is the same brown face everywhere, the same shortcomings, the same pitfalls. And, oh, the things he saw, the things he knew, the things he heard from the drunken lips of whores. Who was good, was there any good face, any good heart that remained so in this crowd?

"Among our countrymen here, we know those that have not yet been touched, and when we see them for the first time, our hearts go out to them, for we know that one day, it will be the same old story all over again, and these good boys will be like us, monkey-faced and coarse, and unfeeling."

"You are not unfeeling, Ambo," I said, wanting to touch his hand.

But he completely ignored me, in the same way that we ignored Leo and Val and their girls. Now they were a bit noisy, especially the girls. Now and then they would come to me and hold my hands and fondle my cheeks, but I said, "Go away. Ambo here is talking"; and Ambo talked on softly, but soberly in the dialect that these two girls didn't understand.

And we still ignored them, even as they started to kiss at our table. The girls were evidently getting tipsy and the boys were a little more talkative and gay.

"That's why the first time I saw you," Ambo was saying when Val interrupted him.

"Ben, has Ambo told you already the hand he held when he ran away, and you won all that cash?"

"No," I said, eager to know, but wanting Ambo to finish what he was saying.

"Go 'way and dance," said Ambo, smiling toward the couples. The waiters walked back and forth; ours was particularly busy, waiting on the girls. Now they were ordering some more.

"Tell him, Ambo," said Val.

"Tell me, Ambo," I said. "You showed your cards to Val. You bluffer, what did you get?"

"Bluffer, he says," said Val, laughing aloud, "tell him, Ambo."

But Ambo wouldn't say anything.

"You won't believe it," said Val, "he had a straight flush."

"Straight flush?" said Leo, pushing away his girl's face.

I looked at Ambo without asking a question. Deep inside me I felt it was true. Then Ambo nodded a little shamefacedly.

"I couldn't understand it," he said. "It never happened before. I thought you would let me alone with that man. I just wanted to bust the other guy; but you kept coming and then when you raised, I looked at my cards. Holy smoke, I got straight flush!"

"And you deliberately gave away the money?"

"Oh, it was really coming to you, Ben," Ambo said.

"By golly," I said, "what made you do it?"

"I like you," he said very simply.

"I like you too," said one of the girls, reaching for my hand.

"Oh, you lovely people!" said the other as she giggled.

I drank what was left of my drinks, for I had suddenly felt thirsty. The couples were dancing again. Ambo's eyes were bloodshot. Had he taken much more than he should?

"You don't know this. It was on a summer day the first time I saw you," Ambo said in a soft, tired voice, "you were sitting with an American friend at the Griffith Stadium. You were eating peanuts, and you looked so flushed and excited, saying, it was your first baseball game in the United States. And you looked so young, I remembered how it was many years ago, we also looked so young. Then you saw me, and our eyes met, and you put forth your bag of peanuts and said, 'Have some.' I shook my head and mumbled my thanks, but you stood and came over, and practically forced me and my other companion to get some. 'They're good peanuts,' you said, and you look like a young brother. And all evening I sat there saying to myself, there are still good boys in this country, but that one, how long will he remain this way?"

In the dim light, Ambo looked like my big brother himself.

Then the couples came back, still hugging each other. Ambo and I sat there awkwardly silent.

"Dance with us," said the girls. And one of them put forth her hands to touch my face, saying, "Why didn't I see it before?" I pushed her hand away. And Ambo said softly in the dialect, "Be gentle."

"I'm sorry," I said to the girl.

"Now you will dance with me," she said. "Come on, beautiful eyes."

"They'll close up soon," said Ambo.

"Let's have another drink," said the other girl.

"It's time to go," said Ambo.

And both girls turned to him and said, "You're mean!" And he smiled at them, saying, "I ain't really bad, babies."

The fresh air outside was good, like one's favorite drink. It was pure like youth that never left home.

"I think I better drive this time," I said.

"Oh, no, you won't," said Ambo. "You have to know these roads by heart like I do."

"Are you sure you can drive . . . now?" I asked.

"You're too very young," Ambo said, getting behind the wheel. The two couples had already settled down in the backseat. And all through the drive, one of the girls kept touching my back and saying a lot of things.

When I arrived in the apartment, it was morning. The blinds were partly drawn and the sunshine lay on the window sill, spilling over in a patch of brightness at the foot of the bed, where Doc lay fast asleep, holding in his hands close to his breast, the picture of a woman, a frail and little woman, with dark trusting eyes.

# OF OTHER DEATHS

*Wednesday evening the boys were at the apartment. Doc and I* were eating when they came. They said that they had just finished having dinner at the *Mei Fu* on 18th Street and Columbia and remembered what fun it would be if they could have desserts with us at the apartment. They remembered a can of peaches and another can of fruit cocktail. There would be ice and ice cream perhaps? It happened there was ice cream.

"It isn't much," I said, "and will do for all of us, unless we allowed Teroy to divide it among us with his own personal sense of proportion."

"I'll divide it in all fairness," he said, "with malice towards none."

But the boys would not let him. By the time they were ready with the peaches and the fruit cocktail, Doc and I were ready for dessert.

Val was brewing coffee. Leo had put ice on the peaches and the fruit cocktail. Now he was setting the saucers and the cups for the ice cream.

"Poor Ben," he said, "but I'll help you with the dishes."

"Mike will do the dishes tonight," I said. He was monkeying with the radio.

"You should have had dinner with us," said Teroy. "We called you up, but you were out."

"We were at the grocery," Doc said.

"It was Leo's party," Teroy explained, "he has just had an article published in this magazine."

"What's it about?" Doc asked, "America, I Love You?"

"Or is it," I added, "hallelujah, hallelujah, we are so happy heah! You can turn out a best-seller on that theme, you know."

"No," said Teroy, "this one is on economics."

"How happy," I said in parody of our good friend Ambo.

"Mike and I say that it's a lot of theories and resounding phraseology that gets the actual economy of a country nowhere. And he says, of course, he says we're just plain dumb. It's so crystal clear to him. But every time he opens his mouth, it's more gruesome theorizing compounded minutely."

"Let's talk about girls," said Val, winking at Doc.

"Girls and economics don't mix," said Mike.

"You should know," I said.

Leo didn't seem to care. He was enjoying his dessert. But after a while, he smoked a cigarette, and turned half-closed eyes towards us in the manner of one who knew better.

"I'm afraid, gentlemen," he announced, "I'm afraid that if the truth be said, it will hurt. You have no background. My article is not for you."

"But we are interested," said Teroy. "Besides, why write a highly technical article? Must readers perspire over your articles, trying to decipher their highly technical language, when what we need is something crystal clear? Our country is suffering from the greatest economic crisis since . . . any time within my memory."

"So what?"

"Don't you see? We need solutions. We expect guidance from those who know. We have no time for cryptograms."

"You're a lawyer," said Leo. "If you write an article on international law for, say, a lawyer's journal, would you expect a man like . . . like Ambo, for instance, to understand it?"

"That's a different story," said Teroy, "but this is not a technical magazine. Besides, whatever you say, big business is on its way back to the Philippines. What am I saying? Why, like MacArthur, it has already returned. And maybe it's all for the best."

Then there were more words exchanged. Quotations from

the article. Leo's hands describing circles; Teroy's fingers flying in the air before his face. Words . . . words . . .

Later Val said, "I understand you've been around, Ben. Why
don't you write about your tour in the United States? That will
make a good book."

And they all pounced upon me, asking why didn't I write a
book about my trip. "You must remember a lot of things,"
they said.

"You bet I remember a lot of things," I said.

"Tell us," they said, "You never told us."

"It isn't a hymn of praise," I said, "how can I have it published in America?"

"You do this country a great injustice," Leo said. "I have
read books making fun of this country. I have never seen a
people with a more wonderful sense of humor."

"But I cannot make fun of it," I said. "I have nothing to tell,
really. What I remember most will not make a book; it will not
even make a song, or a poem. It will be all sensation, all feeling."

"Tell us," they said.

The night had come upon us again. Nothing but empty
hours ahead; and sleep; and then another day.

In Oneonta, I picked apples from the trees and the young
American girls laughed to know that those were my first
apples from the tree. We walked in the rain to a log cabin near
a swollen pond. They pulled down the window shutters and
built fire in the fireplace, and dried their wet boots, and
warmed their hands. And they sang to me their American
songs; and we had coffee and doughnuts; and music from a
phonograph. And we danced on the rugged floor, and they
asked me, "Are all Filipinos like you?" A boy stood in the rain
shooting at the trees near the pond.

In Muncie, I watched young American children frolicking at
a halloween party; and that same night I told a group of girls a
gruesome Philippine ghost story. And there were doughnuts
and cider. In the morning, a little Irish girl named Pat showed
me where the nearest Catholic church was, and left me to my
prayers as she waited outside. "I prayed, too," she said.

We swam at Higgins Lake in Michigan, and we lay on the sand, looking at the sky. Once, I said, our skies are bluer than your skies, and my American friends laughed to hear me say that. We camped by the firelight near the lake, and two colored boys sang spirituals. And I sang a *kundiman* softly, thinking of home.

One week I stayed in Terre Haute, and on leaving, I saw Wanda running through the college campus, waving a book. It was a new edition of Omar Khayyam. She gave me the book. "Goodbye," she said, "and remember us who have not courage enough but are trying hard."

In Emporia, one of the American college girls who was married to a Filipino in Kansas City, took me around the town and showed me her husband's picture: a dark, good looking boy with prominent cheekbones. On my departure, she told me, now she would walk the campus with her head high. "Now, I know," she said "why I love my husband."

In Troy, Alabama, a barefoot freckled boy took me to his house on the farm. The family had a boy in the Philippines. They wanted me to stay for the night there. We had ham and sweet potatoes for dinner and plenty of milk.

A bony, overgrown boy from a farm in Kentucky, carried my suitcases all the way to the station at four o'clock in the morning and refused payment. "You said something yesterday, sir," he drawled, "which I shall remember always."

In Bloomington, Illinois, a whole student body sang our Philippine National Anthem (as we stood in the auditorium) after the "Star Spangled Banner." An old American teacher, who had taught for some years in the Philippines, brought her ancient mother along with her. "I wanted Mother to see," she said, "how the boys we taught in the Philippines had grown up to be."

In a little Spanish village in New Mexico, I sat on the porch, listening to the radio, telling the news of President Roosevelt's death. And I saw tears in the eyes of the peasants who heard the story.

In San Francisco, a Filipino trailed me all night and wanted some money. In Oakland, I met a Filipino pimp. In St. Louis there was a government student who taught dancing and marked his cards. He would not talk of books. Every time he opened his mouth, it was to say how attractive he was to the women. A girl in Stockton told me that her Filipino husband had just been reported killed in action. Now she wondered how she could get the money coming to her. How much did I think it was? Did I know? She had a new boy-friend. Who was my girl-friend? Didn't I think she had shapely legs?

Warm nights in Detroit, crazy days in Chicago, an icy wind blowing forever from the lakes, unbelievable things near the Riverside Drive, in the summer cabins in the north woods, in out of the way places in the Midwest; terrifying poverty near the Ozark mountains, and the great Mississippi River flowing forever; and the lights going on again all over the world.

"Who would publish such things?"

"Nobody," said Mike, "because you remember the wrong things."

"You can write a poem," said Leo.

"I forgot something," I said; "in Shippensburg, the railways passed through the college campus."

"Heaven help you," said Mike "but you remember the wrong things."

There was a knocking on the door. "I'll get it," said Val.

When the door opened, Ambo stood there smiling, his gold teeth sparkling as usual. Beside him stood another Filipino, wearing a vest sweater.

"Come in," I called from the living room. "All the boys are here."

"Good," said Ambo.

The boys met him with loud cheers. Val was wringing his hand. We had learned to miss him, even if only for a day or two. He had been practically with us since the night of our last poker game

"This is Juan Perez, but everybody calls him Johnny. He drove me here in his taxi. You've seen his taxi named Corregidor. That's his."

After 1942, all over the United States the names Bataan, Corregidor, Manila were common sights, on the doors of Filipino club houses and other establishments, in little grocery stores in corners, and in taxis. The names paid in dollars because the

American is a sentimental worshipper of names that stood for something grand like Corregidor, Bataan, Manila. And Filipinos took advantage of it. Even those who came from Batac or Sinait said they came from Bataan, and it paid dividends.

"Can you beat it," said Ambo, "they let us in through the main door?"

"Cut out your kidding," we said.

"That's right," Ambo said, speaking in the dialect, and changing his voice to a near whisper. "Boys, we've come on a sorrowful mission. One of the Filipinos in Washington died this afternoon, a pauper. Now we're going around for contributions to give him a decent burial."

"By golly, that's right," said Teroy. "Even Filipinos die in America. Why do I keep forgetting that? Who was he?"

"Chavez. Nanoy he is called," Ambo replied sadly. "I knew him very well. He was a good boy. He came to America to study. He was unlucky."

"What did he die of?" Doc asked.

"Cancer, I think," said Ambo.

"Some say it's T.B.," Johnny said.

"Do they also die in New York?" Teroy asked.

"Everywhere," said Val.

"Why do I keep forgetting that?" said Teroy as though talking to himself. "Yes we can also die in America," he added as though it were a brilliant idea.

"We usually go around like this," Ambo explained, "because the boys often die destitute. Medicines, doctors, etc., take up all their savings, if they had any savings at all. When they die we take care that they are decently buried. This is the first time I've come for your help because I didn't know you too well before. I'm sure you've not heard of other deaths."

We had not. Now we gave liberally and Ambo and the other boy looked very much pleased.

"Will there be a sort of funeral?" asked Mike.

"Most of the taxi boys follow the hearse to the cemetery on the hill outside the city."

"When will this be?" I asked.

"Tomorrow at four in the afternoon."

"We are going," Leo said. "Teroy and I will have our cars at your disposal. If the boys need any help, please tell us."

Ambo was grateful and seemed happy. He looked at us with pride in his eyes, and something more than the sparkle of gold in his smile.

"Are you sure you wanted to attend the funeral, Leo?" Teroy asked.

"Of course," said Leo. "Why do you ask?"

"I was just asking."

Mike turned on the radio.

# LONELY IN THE AUTUMN EVENING

*Ambo and I sat together in the backseat in Teroy's car. We were* four or five cars behind the black Cadillac with the coffin. All the cars had their headlights on as though it were night.

Ambo was talking in the dialect telling the story of the dead Nanoy.

Deep in your heart, Ben, do you really think so? Do they truly remember us yet, the loved ones we left behind in the old hometown? Perhaps in the beginning yes. But after a long while, when letters have gradually become far apart, containing nothing, hiding so much; or after they have ceased altogether and the years have clamped down the silence of space and time, would they still care? Yes, Mother perhaps. But Mother would not be living now. And Nanoy's mother died the year he left on a ship bound for Tacoma.

Yes, yes, Mothers perhaps. They will not forget. Their memory of us will always be as green as June . . . a defiant boy with a will of his own, soiling his clothes in the mud . . . panting for breath after a race in the cornfields . . . rubbing tears away from dirty cheeks . . . a little tousled head upon the lap. But it is the sort of remembering that we their sons do not deserve.

What am I talking about? As if we deserved anything better than this. As the years pass by, in the home of our young manhood, we become nothing but a name mentioned now and then, casually, and always, without love; a blurred face in a picture fast yellowing with the years; then completely unrecognizable in some family album, or on a wall among a hundred other faces. Or if someone remembered still, those whom we knew, those with whom we were young, would say, yes, yes, he left for the States many years ago. Maybe he's dead now, or maybe he's still around, standing in some shady corner of a despised city. Then everybody would be talking for a while, giving many reasons why he left.

Nanoy left because of some woman. Rather, because of his father. My father, he said, couldn't think of anything else but money, and the girl was poor and I was a coward. Nanoy had never forgiven his father. Many times he wept like a child about his exile. He was very young when he came. He had rosy cheeks and a mane of dark wavy hair; and even when he talked in anger, his dimples showed. As we walked Kearny Street in Frisco, he would sometimes get lost in the thick fog, and he would hold out his hand, calling my name like a lost child. I have seen many a child like him since, lost in a thousand fogs of the big and the small cities of this country. Those are the stories for you, Ben, but they are sad stories. All our stories are sad.

But I keep thinking of home, Ben. How would they know out there of our passing? Would we come to them in a dream, speak to them out of a cloud, and tell them goodbye, we have just passed away? No? Then perhaps, suddenly in the midst of a day's work on the farm, or silent in the old wooden house by the sea, our name would mingle with their thoughts. Or perhaps it would seem as though some one passed by and he looked like us, a remembered movement of the head, a manner of walking, or a flash of likeness in a stranger's face.

But it is better that nobody remembers. It is well that nobody knows. Nanoy's life was a slow moving towards an end that meant the inevitable gutter and the filth. If someone told me years ago when I first knew him that that boy with the flushed cheeks and the clean eyes would end up in a vermin-infested room in the colored section near the wharf by the Potomac, I would have called him a liar.

But that was the truth. He shared a room in the basement with a colored janitor. The walls were untidy and cracked. Insects crawled all over the place. It reeked with the smell of urine and human waste. He was already dead when we came. He never knew that we had seen his place. The few times we would see him hanging around the Club, he wouldn't say where he was staying. Sometimes he dropped the hint that he was in a Maryland sanitarium.

He lay on a cot, partly covered with what seemed to have been an Ilocano blanket. He didn't leave anything behind him. "Last week," said the janitor, "he gave me his suitcase. My rent, he says, and I says, keep it, but he won't hear of no such thing. Told me to burn everything."

Even the picture of his boy must have been burned. He had a boy, you know. I called him Donald Duck for he had a voice that sounded like Donald Duck's. Nanoy came with him from Chicago. I never saw the wife, but they tell me she was tall and haughty. She hated her son because she had to take care of him. One day she ran away. No, she didn't really run away. She just left. One evening when Nanoy came home from work, tired and greasy, she waited for him till after he had bathed and changed, and she told him. "Nanoy," she said, "I don't love you any more. I'm leaving, you may have Junior." And she left.

I'm sure he cried. For even after the years should have hardened him, he was still the same Nanoy I knew, getting lost in the fog and stretching out his hands and calling for help. He was weak. Where another man would have held the woman and made her stay, he must have done nothing at all but plead with her and plead in vain.

Nanoy came over to Washington. Junior was a fine little boy, not more than five years old. He had his father's face and his mother's brown hair. Nanoy worked on odd jobs, leaving the boy with some family, or to some charitable church people who took care of the children of working parents.

When he got himself a taxi, he would cruise about with Junior beside him; but the boy could not stand that sort of thing, especially in winter. Sometimes he would leave the boy to play with the children of Filipino-American couples on 4th Street. Even if his fare didn't have to pass by there he would make a detour just to be able to see his boy playing. The other children would shout, "Your daddy!" and Junior would squeal with delight, and Nanoy would wave his hand, slowing the taxi a little. Sometimes, if his passenger was in no hurry and looked kind, he would stop and talk to Junior.

Nanoy was not very healthy when he came to Washington. Taxi driving was too much for him. He had to be sent to the sanitarium, but there was nobody to take care of Junior. The child was himself very sickly. He always had a running nose, and very often his skin was infested with sores. Parents kept their children away from him. Nanoy knew this and it made him sad.

At around Christmas time, Nanoy had not yet found anyone who would take care of his son. It was a severe winter. Nanoy had not been to work regularly. He carried the boy in his arms and went from house to house among our countrymen, looking for someone who would take care of Junior for him while he stayed in the sanitarium. "I will get well soon," he promised. "And Junior is a good boy. Aren't you, Junior?"

Before the winter was over, the little boy had passed away. He died in a hospital for orphan children. Nanoy himself was in the hospital then. We tried to keep the news from him, but he learned of it. "I knew it," he said. "I have a picture of Junior here. The day he died, there was a changed expression on the boy's face. He died also in his picture. I knew it. I knew it."

And when they buried Nanoy, the wind was blowing from the river across the hillock where a group of us stood bareheaded under a dark September sky. A wooden cross painted white, bore his name and the date of his passing. Nobody spoke and our heads were bowed in grief. I looked at the mud sticking to my shoes. It was reddish brown and soft, like earth on a hillock after the rain. I have seen such earth before, in the muddy fields among the Sinicaran hills in Albay, along the muddy trails in June beneath the church of Antopolo. But as we walked away and I looked back, a dark smoke floated above the dying trees in the graveyard wind-borne from a dozen chimneys of a sprawling ammunitions factory. Nanoy's grave stood lonely in the autumn evening.

# THE DOOR

*Oh, the stories I can tell you, if you but have the time to listen, but* you are going away. Everybody is going some place. They are all in a hurry, they will not listen to me. And those who will tarry here forever, they have no ears for my stories, because they have seen them happen everywhere, and they don't want them told, they are a commonplace, they say, they should be hushed and forgotten. We have had happy moments which, truly, had not quite lasted but there will be other such moments. So my friends will not listen, because my tales are sad, because they do not have the heart.

But you will listen to me, Ben, even if you too are going away. Because I saw the look in your eyes as you turned around to gaze at Nanoy's grave; and I knew that you too could have loved Nanoy and shared his loneliness, you could have suffered in your heart as we that loved him had suffered. So I walked beside you and held your hand, and deep in my heart I felt, Ben will understand my stories, to him I shall tell them.

*i*

In our apartment, there were four of us. I was happy with my friends, because everybody spoke my language, our language, I feel so happy using it now with you. We spoke in English only when we cursed, it came in so nicely. Or when another countryman dropped in for a chat, and he kept talking in English, then the other boys talked, too. They talked very well, and all I would say was, "Yes," or "Hell, that's a fact," in an attempt to cover up my terrible ignorance which my rough trembling hands so often exposed.

There were other boys and Filipino families in the apartment building. I knew Delfin because I often met him near the stair landing. His room was just across the way, at the foot of the staircase. Here he lived with Mildred, his blonde American wife and her two little daughters, Anne and Esther, by a previous marriage.

I was very fond of the two little girls because they were so pretty and little and they had such curly golden hair. Soon they were calling me Uncle. Often I brought them candy bars and they would rush to meet me near the main door of the apartment building. I put my arms round their wet sticky necks and gave them what I had remembered to buy. Mildred would scold them sometimes, saying nasty things. She would come out of the door wearing a silk negligee and she would run after them in the hall as they squealed and cried and ran away from her. "You spoil their appetites," Mildred would tell me, and I would answer in English, of course, "It don't matter none, really," I said. Delfin would sometimes be around watching the chase. All he would do was smile stupidly and look on. He never invited me to his apartment. Often I would stand near the open door and talk with the little girls. That was all.

One day I heard the boys in our apartment talking about Delfin. I was surprised at the things they said about him. Dick, Noli, and Sev seldom agreed on many things, but they were one in their condemnation of Delfin. It wouldn't have been for meanness. My friends were not angels, but they led such busy lives that they had no time to sprout wings or grow horns. It must be true then, the things they said.

"You don't know him yet, Ambo," said Dick, "but wait till you do, and then you would be saying the same things that you hear us saying now." Dick had finished law school, working days and studying at night. He was very gentle by nature, and wouldn't be talking of another man this way if it was not a fact that Delfin was everything they said about him.

"He's a disgrace to our people," said loud-mouthed Noli, for whom everything was country and politics. He had a shrill voice and wanted to be a Senator in the Philippines. He was intensely nationalistic. Everything a Filipino did in America was a reflection on our country and our people.

"Delfin's a damn fool," was Sev's private opinion. Sev drove a taxi. He was neat and effeminate in his ways. His taxi was adorned with pictures of the Lady of Lourdes, of all sizes. There were also pictures of MacArthur and the American and Filipino flags intertwined as if in lovingness.

It seemed that it was common knowledge that Mildred ran around with other boys. She would take them to her apartment, and Delfin would leave quietly and walk the streets. If he was not home and came later, and he would find the door locked from the inside, he knew that he had come at the wrong time again. He would wait outside the apartment building, till a strange man came out, and he would try the door again with his key. Often he slept elsewhere, especially on winter nights when walking up and down the streets or loafing in badly heated hamburger joints made him sick—a shooting pain through the meat of his legs or through the stoop of his back. He would go to our apartment. He would knock at our door at the most unholy hours of the night and say, "May I sleep here tonight?"

The boys would let him in the living room, show him the couch and throw him a blanket. Dick and Sev would pretend to be very sleepy, for they hated to see him that way, as though the thing were happening to them, too. But if Noli was awake, he would shout from his room, "Is that you again, Del? God, you're not a man. You must have been castrated in childhood. Why don't you leave that woman? Why do you make a goddamn fool of yourself? She's beautiful. All right. Aren't there others as willing, less shameless? Man, where's your sense of honor? We're ashamed of you! If you don't listen to us, why come here at all? You insult us with your presence. You contaminate us with your . . . with your . . . filth!"

Delfin would pull the blanket over him, as if to shut off the words a little and the light from the street lamp below. Then he would be quiet as though fast asleep.

Once when Delfin came to our apartment, the boys told him stories of men who defended their honor.

Sev said, "Have you heard of the Filipino in St. Louis who caught his wife sleeping with another man? He chased the man through the streets. The man was naked and held a pillow close to his breast as if that protected him. He was so scared. Then the Filipino went back to his wife and slashed her throat." Sev made a slashing motion with his hands across his throat, then a choking sound. It was picturesque. It was gruesome.

"And after he had slashed her throat," Sev continued, "he cut off her nipples. Then he gave himself up, carrying the nipples in his hands, staining the sergeant's blotter with blood. He's now in an insane asylum."

Dick had the kindness of heart to change the subject. Meanwhile Delfin hadn't said a word in his defense, but he clung to every word of the storyteller, and he swallowed a little near the end. Then when everybody was quiet, he said, "I don't think I can kill Mildred. I don't think I can live without her." His sincerity touched us all. For the first time I saw Noli look at him without contempt, but with pity, with a little kindness.

I was coming home late after midnight in October when I found Delfin sitting on the stone steps of our apartment building, his head against the stone pillar.

"You frightened me," I said as soon as I was sure that it was he. Delfin had a young face. He was tall and very dark. His teeth sparkled whitely when he smiled. And he was smiling now.

"Did you have a good time?" he asked, and without waiting for a reply, he added, "Sit down a while with me. It's too warm inside."

"You're not staying here all night, are you?" I asked, sitting down on the cold stone steps.

"Oh, no," he said, looking in the direction of their apartment.

"You got a visitor?" I tried with difficulty to make my question sound matter-of-fact.

His answer was a slight nod of the head.

"Man," I said, "You're crazy."

"I know," he said softly.

This would go on. I would be saying a lot of things that wouldn't mean anything to him. So I asked after Anne and Esther. Were they all right? Of course, they were all right. What did the little ones know? God, why did they have to know? God, why did I stay there, sitting down on the cold stone steps, sharing these crazy hours of waiting with a man like Delfin? A terrible anger was welling up inside me: all I wanted to do was try to understand.

"Let's go upstairs to our apartment," I said. "It's getting chilly out here."

"No," he said. "Noli's just come up. He told me not to go to your apartment tonight or else he would throw me out."

"That would serve you right," I said, clenching my fist, getting all of Noli's anger in me.

"Hell!" I cried impulsively, jumping to my feet. "Let's go to your apartment. We'll bust the door and take the . . . out of both of them."

"No," said Delfin, "you will wake up the little girls."

I stared at him for a while, spitting at the pavement at my feet. Then I sat down again and laughed softly. What had got into me? What business did I have straightening, so to say, the back-hanging collar of this cuckold of a man, countryman or no countryman?

"Oh, well," I said after a while, "I guess you know best."

"No," he admitted. "I'm all wrong. I'm all sick inside of me, worse than leprosy."

"You know," I said, "there are many nice girls at the Club."

"I know."

"Some of them a lot better looking than Mildred. And a million times nicer."

"How do you know?"

"I don't. But I know Mildred."

"I love Mildred."

"Love, my God! What do you know of love? It's a curse; it's a disease that has got into you."

"I know. I know. I told you it's worse than leprosy. But sometimes I tell myself it's love. We called it love in the beginning. We have moments of beauty together, Mildred and

I, and I find this nowhere else. No other woman could give it to me. I cannot live without her, I tell you. I can't . . . I can't."

He held his head in his hands and he was quiet. I sat there, looking at him, and thinking: Lord, the things Filipinos do in this country. The things we say. The things that happen to us. What keeps us living on like this from day to day, from loveless kiss to loveless kiss, from venomed touch to venomed touch. Thrill of the gaming table, what keeps us alive, thrill of a woman's arms, sight of her body, sharp fleeting moments of dying . . . they are the blessed ones like Nanoy, though it took him too long to die.

Busy with these thoughts, I had not noticed a man leave the building. Now only his back was visible in the street light beyond. His steps were brisk and fast as though already late.

"Was that the man?" I asked.

"I don't know," Delfin answered. "I don't know any one of them."

Then we stood up, and together we walked through the hallway, pausing in front of his apartment. The door was closed still. Delfin placed his hand upon it, and it opened quietly to his touch.

"Goodnight," he said, his teeth sparkling in a happy smile.

I went up to my room, groping in the dark. Someone had turned off the stairway light again. Now I would have to fumble for the lock on our door, or maybe it would yield to my touch like magic.

*ii*

It was not often during these many years in America that I could look forward to a Christmas with honest joy. Christmas to me was just another day. It meant more people spending money, bigger tips, and the spoken words, "Merry Christmas." It meant that there would be more boys at the club, more little men at the races. It meant silly talks in corners, at lonely tables in Filipino restaurants: "Last night I dreamed I was back home in the Philippines and it was Christmas. Sister was a grown up lady. She was wearing an afternoon dress I had bought at Hecht's. She was lovely, like my memory of

Mother when I was a child. There was a whole platter full of rice cakes, *suman* wrapped in yellow leaves. The air was full of the smell of roasting pigs. And many little children came to me and kissed my hand. In each of their palms I placed a new silver dollar—I had a bagful from Riggs National Bank—you should have seen the glitter of the silver under the lamplight; you should have seen the glitter in the children's eyes."

Sometimes Christmas meant walking up and down the icy streets, looking for a restaurant, and finding none, for most of them are closed on Christmas Day. Because most people should be home on Christmas instead of walking up and down the streets, with icy winds blowing from the River, their steps swinging to the music of Christmas carols, sung everywhere, loudest in the crowded streets above the din of hurried steps turned towards home; megaphones blaring forth joy to the world, the Lord is come. But, please Lord, let me find a place where I could eat. I'm so hungry.

But I looked forward to that Christmas with honest joy. For the first time in many years, I had a Christmas gift for someone, for two little blonde girls who called me Uncle.

Once I had fever and I kept to my room. Every time the boys came from work, the first thing they said, invariably, was, "Anne and Esther want to know how you are."

On the third day, the two little girls came to my room crying. "Mom would not let us see you," they said. "But now she's away. Get well quick, Uncle," they pleaded.

Anne put her little soft hands on my forehead. "Do you have a headache?" she said.

"A little," I said, truthfully. She passed her fingers across my forehead, lightly, gently.

Little Esther said, "I'll rub your legs."

"Don't," I said, "that will tickle me." And we three laughed.

After a while, I said, "You'd better go now." And they kissed me goodbye. When they had gone, I turned to the wall and closed my eyes.

And one day, shortly before Christmas, the two little girls came up to me, crying, "Uncle, Uncle, we've a Christmas tree!"

They opened the door of their apartment wide enough for us

to see across the hall in a corner: a pretty, lighted Christmas tree.

The next day I got busy asking friends what I could give for Christmas to two little girls. There were a number of suggestions. Different persons told me different things. I spent the next few days, walking through F Street, between 7th and 14th Streets, looking for an apt gift for each child. And I was happy within me. For the first time in many years, there was a glow in my heart, Christmas felt truly like Christmas, and the songs in the streets, and the carols in the air, and the little tinkling bell in the hand of the Salvation Army man or woman now freezing in the cold—all had meaning.

As soon as I had their gifts packed nicely, one for Anne and the other for Esther, I attached a little print card decorated with holly on each, and wrote "Merry Christmas." My hand didn't seem heavy and my heart was light; there was no hesitancy, no sluggishness in the movement of my hand as I wrote on each, "Love, Uncle," as though my hand for such things need not have to tremble, since there was nothing to hide, and something deep to say, which I was just saying now, after these many years, love to you, to anyone, this time to two little girls with windblown curls and the prettiest freckled noses you ever saw.

I gave the two little packages to Mildred. She stood by the open door and received them from me. "For their stockings," I said.

"Anne and Esther have also something for you," Mildred said.

And I stood at the open door wondering what it was that tugged at my heart, like the singing of many happy voices that have not had voice nor music for a long, long time.

On Christmas eve I went down after dinner and the little girls were there awaiting me. I stood by the open door while their hands held mine, pulling me into the room.

"Where's Del?" I asked.

"He's working tonight," said Mildred. She stood in the hall, slim and attractive in a red housecoat. She was combing back her yellow curls. "I've just had a bath," she said as though to apologize. She exuded soap and orange blossoms.

"Merry Christmas," I said as I allowed myself to be pulled in by the two very eager girls.

"Nice Christmas tree," I said.

"The winkers don't work," said Mildred. She showed me a box of winkers that she said she had been trying to use.

I fixed the socket and the wire ends, and turned on the juice, but they wouldn't work. I sat on the rug and fixed the wiring. Then Esther went to the door and came back, saying, "I've closed the door. Uncle is staying with us tonight." Anne was also saying something else. Mildred had turned on the radio and there was loud singing. I heard Esther's words, but I didn't bother to weigh their meaning. Mildred watched me as I worked, and she, too, knelt playfully on the rug and puttered around the Christmas tree. The little girls were dancing about and singing.

Soon I turned on the juice again and the winkers came on and went off in a glorious moment that seemed success, and the two little girls gave out a cry of happiness. It was short-lived, because the winkers didn't come on any more, and I was beginning to get embarrassed about my inability to do anything about them.

"We shouldn't have put them on too early," Mildred explained, and in a resigned voice, added, "they're really no good though. The other lights will do."

"But we like the winkers, Mom," the girls cried. And they urged me to keep on trying.

So I spent several minutes more, tinkering with the wire ends. I was getting hot round the neck, so I said, "Mind if I take this off?" and I removed my jacket, and the girls ran away with it to their room.

"Be careful!" Mildred shouted after them. She turned to me and asked, "Isn't there anything important in your pockets?"

"No," I said without looking up from my work.

Well, by the time the winkers were good and working, it was nearly bedtime for the little ones. The whoop of delight with which they announced my success was not as loud nor as vociferous as their first, though protracted, yell of delight earlier in the night.

Anne gave a Christmas poem about a silent house without

noise, and without a mouse, but she kept yawning and forgetting the lines, we had to clap our hands before she was through. Then Esther sang "Silent Night" and Mildred and Anne joined her; and I kept humming, too, and it seemed, I had always known the melody without having been aware of it.

"Now you'll go to bed like good girls," said Mildred, "And Santa Claus will fill your stockings with gifts."

"Yes, Mom," they said sleepily as they pulled me to their bedroom. It was a pretty bedroom, done up in blue and red. There was a bed where they slept side by side. Over the wall that looked like a fireplace, they had hung two empty stockings.

"That's mine," said Esther.

"This is mine," said Anne.

Mildred pulled Esther to her and started dressing her for the night.

"Help me," said Anne, getting up on a chair. And I helped her, a little awkwardly at first.

"Thank you," said Anne, putting her arms around me impulsively, and nearly falling off the chair. Then she kissed me hard on the cheek, saying, "Goodnight, Uncle."

"Goodnight," said Esther, pulling me down to her. And she kissed me on the cheek, less fervently, sleepily.

"It's beyond their sleeping time," said Mildred, as she turned off the light and closed the door after us.

"I have my jacket there," I said.

"It's all right," said Mildred. "What about a midnight snack?"

I turned the radio low as Mildred got busy in the kitchen.

"What would you have?" she asked.

"Anything," I said, going to the kitchen. "I'm not really hungry."

"The kitchen is a mess," she apologized. Then she added, "Del should be here by now. It's past midnight. I wonder what's detaining him?"

Mildred placed a couple of sandwiches before me and a bottle of cold milk. She sat at the end of the table with a glass of milk.

"Spending Christmas with the boys, I suppose?" she said.

"Maybe," I said, not really having any plans.

"Did you know Del quite well before you came to America? He talks a great deal about you. It seems, your people knew each other quite well."

"Yes," I said, lying deliberately. When we talked of boys we liked to our American friends, we always said we knew each other in the Philippines; and we talked about our families as though we had deep ties of association and kinship. Mostly it was just talk. Perhaps it gave us strength to talk like that. We didn't want to appear the homeless waifs that we were. We didn't wish to be known as the forgotten children of long lost mothers and fathers, as grown up men without childhood, bastards of an indifferent country.

"Yes," I repeated, "We knew each other very well," adding another deliberate lie: "His family was well known in our province. His father was tall and dark like him, and deeply loved by all. Del's father was noble."

"And his Mother?" Mildred asked. "He talked of her more often."

"She was a sweet lady. She was loving and religious. She was faithful."

"Do you want another glass of milk?" Mildred asked.

"No, thanks," I said, "I'd better be going. Must be past midnight now."

"I'll get your jacket," she said.

When she came out of the girls' bedroom, she had the jacket in her hands.

"Let me help you," she said.

"No, thanks," I said, taking the jacket gently from her hand, and folding it. "I'm just going up like this."

"Well, it's Christmas Day," Mildred said, giving me her hand, "Merry Christmas, Ambo."

"Thanks," I said. "Merry Christmas also." I let go of her hand quickly. Mine were trembling so.

"Anne and Esther make me very happy," I said. It was a great truth that I had to say.

"They love you very much," Mildred said, undoing the bar, "I never bolt this door except . . ."

As the door opened, we saw Delfin sitting on the stairway, his head in his hands. Now he looked up at the sound of the opening door, and when he saw me, he stared hard and long. Then he looked away and bit his lips.

"How long have you been sitting there?" Mildred asked him. "Come on in."

Delfin had not moved. He was looking at me still with deep upbraiding eyes.

"Merry Christmas, Del," I said, trying to be casual. What else could I tell him, what could I say? Did I not sit up with him on a night in autumn, while the door to this apartment remained bolted from the inside?

Now he had hidden his head in his hands, and when he looked at me again, his face was contorted as in pain. I wanted to give him my hand, but it lay heavy on my side, my trembling fingers clawing at the folds of my woolen jacket. With great effort, he stood up in answer to Mildred's now insistent bidding, and as he came to my side, a great sadness was on his face, no longer pain, and tears stood in his bloodshot eyes. In a vague whisper, he said, in the dialect, "Why you also, Ambo?"

Then he went in, and the door closed upon them.

Instead of going up to my room as I had intended, I put on my jacket and went outside. It was a cold night; an icy breeze was blowing. But I walked on and on. Then the bells of St. Mary's on Fourth Street began pealing loudly, but the spirit of Christmas had already gone out of me, all the songs, all the music, all the singing gladness within me, all memory of ringing bells.

# FOR THESE RUINS

*It surprised me to see Pablo Icarañgal at the shipping agent's of-*fice in San Francisco when all along I thought he was in Washington. He was glad to see me. At the time, he was having difficulty making himself understood by the clerk. An old-timer in Washington, Pablo had not quite mastered the language. His pronunciation, not to mention his grammar, was as unique as it was incomprehensible. But his friends took his failing as a matter of course as they did his goodness or, say, his trembling hands.

There were a few Filipinos in the shipping office. Among them was a plain looking woman with a child asleep on her shoulder. The child's complexion was light; his hair was almost blonde.

Pablo was insistent that we take the same stateroom. He helped me get a lower bunk beside his, and piled my luggage with his own. In the crowded ship, it was not easy to find a safe place for one's things.

There were no friends to see us off, but Pablo stood at the railing, at departure time, smiling at the crowd, waving his hand, as though everybody had come to bid him good-bye. As soon as the gangplank was removed, I went over to a deck chair and lay down, folding my heavy coat on my lap.

My thoughts should have been of home, the devastated country whose ruins I had read about and seen in newspapers and movies in America, but now as I sat there in the foggy evening, looking at the mist that hung over San Francisco Bay

98

and felt the boat edge away from the pier, I was thinking of the country I was leaving behind me, which had been my home during the war years. I was thinking of the many cities and towns I had walked through, the men and the women who had talked to me, those who had been kind. The schools I went to, the men with whom I sat in English seminars, young and straight and good. Men who became soldiers and were gone. The girls without fellows who took it all with courage or despair. The young widows, the gray-haired mothers, and the thin old men whom the war had touched deeply, for whom a silver star on the window was both a laurel and a cross.

Then it was not persons or places, names of cities hard to spell, harder to pronounce, but corners of streets, rooms and parks, and shades of trees.

And moments. Graduation time and you, looking around for someone to shake your hand; Christmas in far-off places; New Year's Eve without music and the tinkle of ice on glass or wine drops staining white table linen.

Or the way a pretty American girl stared at your brown body, many questions in her eyes, never answered. . . .

"So there you are," the voice was loud and the words were in the dialect. Pablo was standing beside me, saying, "You will freeze to death here. Were you asleep?"

"I think so," I replied, suddenly feeling the chill of the night air. I stood up swaying a little, as I put the heavy coat around me.

I looked towards the land where a hill loomed against the sky sprinkled with stars, but hazy in the distance and the mist.

At our table in the dining room that night were some of the men with whom we shared the stateroom. Two of them, a lawyer and a businessman, were with their wives. There was also a young man named Asistio Salazar, a government student pensionado who had specialized in lip reading. At the other tables were Americans and a group of Filipino army officers. Some of the Americans were old. These were former prisoners of war at Santo Tomas and Cabanatuan, who were now returning to the Philippines after a rest cure in the United States. Several young American boys and girls in the uniform of a traveling troupe of artists were on their way to the East to entertain lonely soldiers with their songs and their dancing. In the crowded dining room were a few mestizos and mestizas. At a table in a corner sat three Filipino priests.

Later a shabby Filipino woman came in. She had a little boy in her arms. She didn't seem to know where she was to be seated until a steward came over and led her to a table. I remembered seeing that woman in the shipping office in San Francisco. She was wearing the same dress, a loose brown woolen that was quite faded. Her hair was unkempt.

"She cannot even comb her hair," the lawyer's wife was saying: "The boy is very fastidious and demands her attention all the time."

Everybody appeared to be talking about her. From what I heard, I began to recall the story of the woman which had recently appeared in *Time* magazine. There was a picture of her and the child. I remembered now.

The name was Julia Flores, from Bataan. During the fighting in the peninsula, she saved the life of a young G.I. The imagination could fill the gaps in the story: A young American soldier lies dying and this girl comes by. She takes care of him through fever and delirium. She is only an illiterate peasant girl of an inland village, but she nurses him back to life. She hides him from the enemy, risking her life and enslaving herself for him. She searches the hills and the rivers for food. Many a night she listens to his dreams and his nightmares. Understanding but little, perhaps nothing at all; fanning his flushed face, cooling his brow with spring water. And in the village, always in hiding, they live together as man and wife, and a son is born to them. Then the war is over. And the soldier-lover takes her along as his wife in gratitude if not in love.

In America, the parents of the boy welcome their long lost son, but they are shocked by the presence of this colored woman, uncouth and unclean, who can only smile like a stupid pagan eager for trinkets, as she extends towards them little Jimmy squirming in her arm. One day Julia finds her husband gone and his family tells her to leave. So she goes away with little Jimmy, packing all her belongings, mostly her little son's, in a duffle bag that once belonged to her husband. The Red Cross comes to help. She and her boy are given passage back to Bataan. (There are many ways of coming back. There is the way of the hero or of the saint, the prodigal, the penitent. This is one other way.) *And so, goodbye, Jim. It was not right for me to have come along with you, but in my simple mind, I thought you needed me still. And thanks for not taking little Jimmy away from me. He will grow up among our hills. Remember? I would wash clothes on the river bank and you would sit on the sand, holding little Jimmy in your arms, teaching him the language neither he nor I ever learned. There was too little time. In my own way, I had loved you, Jim. Perhaps, one day, I will yet understand . . .*

We had fun the first few nights out when the strain of the voyage had not yet quite come upon us. The two husbands in our room were worried over their wives who were seasick and needed them at their side, but they could not stay with them all night. The ship was, in the words of Salazar, "strictly not co-educational." But we noticed that their bunks were nearest the door and kidded them about intending to steal away in the night to join their wives.

"But be careful you don't stumble in the dark against a priest," said Salazar, "You'd have to be married all over again."

Even Pablo who didn't like the student too much, laughed at this joke. We had fun.

Long after we had switched off the lights, in the half-darkness we kept talking and laughing at the things we said as though the stateroom was not for sleeping but for holding confidential sessions on matters as intimate as ambition or an illicit experience. The lawyer was going to practice in Manila. There had been much trouble and confusion. A lawyer like him would have many clients. There would be litigations without end, involving thousands of pesos, maybe millions.

"In two years, at the most, I expect to be established," he said.

The businessman had brought along with him aboard a huge stock of toys and there would be subsequent shipments. "There will be no toys from Japan for a long time and our children must have toys again. They have had nothing to play with all these years," he said.

"Me," said Salazar, "I won't make money. I'm not a money-maker. I've come home to make the dumb talk and the deaf hear."

Pablo spoke in the dialect as usual and he told us about the lands he was going to buy and till; and the wife he was coming home to.

I had no plans myself. The letters I had received from home mentioned a lot of sad things that were not for me to say.

We kept talking beyond midnight. There was always something to say, a moment remembered, a hope that came up more alive after every repetition. But shortly before dawn, Pablo was awake, sitting on his bunk, his head bowed as in prayer.

"Awake already, Pablo?" I asked in a whisper.

"I couldn't sleep," he said, sitting on the edge of my bunk. He spoke so softly I could hardly hear him with the waves dashing under us and the purr of the engines sounding loudly to my unaccustomed ears.

"What's the matter?" I asked.

"I've been thinking about my wife. I've told you about her in Washington. You have seen her picture, haven't you?"

"Oh, yes, I have," I said, remembering the picture of a young pretty Visayan girl in a nurse's uniform. "She's a nurse, isn't she?"

What Pablo was trying to say was that immediately after the American landing in Tacloban, he had been sending her money, telling her that he was coming home on the first boat. Although she mentioned receiving the money, she did not seem eager to see him.

"How do you know she isn't?" I asked.

"Well, she didn't say she was happy I was coming. She didn't say she missed me. She even said, maybe I wouldn't like our old place any more. Now, tell me, has she perhaps fooled around?"

"You're crazy. Better go back to bed and sleep," I said.

"God," he murmured as he lay down. "She wrote such sweet letters before the war."

Before the end of the first week, quite a few passengers failed to show up at the dining room. Once when Pablo and I were alone at supper time, he said, "I can never learn to feel at home in swanky places like this. I never bothered about table manners in America. You know why. Mostly I ate by myself. Hurriedly. And my hands keep trembling, you know, I'm ashamed of them."

I knew those trembling hands. Without looking at them, I could feel the tough palms; the calloused fingers and the stubbed nails. Every time he had held on to something, his hands trembled. Now I was aware how his spoon and fork kept hitting the plate and his teeth with a sickening clatter. But I assured him that nobody noticed his hands, no one paid any attention, none cared.

"Don't be too damn self-conscious," I said.

"You can say that," he said, his spoon falling away from his hold loudly on the plate, "because you have nothing to hide."

The time passed slowly. After Honolulu, there was more sunshine. Except in the early morning and at night, we could walk about on the deck in shirt and slacks. Julia Flores remained in her room, even had her meals taken there. "She feels better alone," the lawyer's wife said. "She feeds the boy and herself with her hand."

One night Pablo came to our room and said, "I skinned them," as he pulled rolls of dollar bills from his pocket. He had been playing with the crew again, and, as usual, won.

"You're lucky," I told him recalling the poker sessions with the boys in Washington on winter nights.

"Lucky in cards, unlucky in love," said Salazar.

"What do you mean?" Pablo asked.

"Just that," said Salazar. "You have a young wife in the Visayas. Suppose when you arrive home, you find that she has several Jap-looking kids?"

I glanced towards Pablo with apprehension. But he was smiling. "I'll give you one of them," he was telling the student. "I'll give you the sickly one. The others, I'll use them to plow my fields."

The lawyer and the businessman roared with laughter.

"But what will you do with your wife?" the student asked.

"I'll give her my own sons. And when they're old enough, I'll send them to America, but not to study like you have studied."

"Oh, so!"

"No, sir. They'll not have your kind of education. I have heard you talk. Every time you open your mouth, you speak of women. Blondes. Blondes. All the time. You're blonde crazy."

"Well," the young man said. "Can I help it if they like me?"

"Oh, sure," said Pablo, "the blondes like you. The blondes you knew liked any guy with two dollars, or is it less where you come from?"

The argument ended up with the student challenging Pablo to a game of poker. Pablo declined, saying, "I pity you. Keep your money, paisano. You'll need it where you are going."

I never saw the student talk to Pablo again after that for the rest of the trip.

But that same night, Pablo was restless in his bunk. Long before morning, when he heard me stir, he came over to me.

"Do you think my wife really got some Jap kid?" he asked in a whisper.

"Shut up," I said, pushing him away. Then I turned on my side, away from him.

In a few more days we expected to see land. Already birds soared over the ship and skimmed over the waves with grace. We kept our eyes in the distance, imagining specks on the horizon where there were none.

One morning when I woke up, Pablo was not in his bunk. I met him only at breakfast. He was looking fine. He told me he had just heard mass.

"I went to confession and had communion," he said.

"Good for you,' I said.

"Why don't you do the same?" he asked. "In Washington, if I remember right, you preferred cathedrals."

"Oh, no. I didn't," I said embarrassed.

I thought the priests on board said masses on Sundays only. So there was mass every morning. I had been wanting to go to confession myself. Many times I passed in front of the open door of the room where the priests stayed. I walked back and forth. Sometimes, one of them would look up from his book and smile at me, but I could not find the courage to speak up and say, "Father, I want to confess."

Then one morning, soon afterwards, I woke up to a great noise in the stateroom. Pablo and the others were crowding round the porthole, talking excitedly.

"Are we there now?" I asked, sitting up. I had heard talk before I went to bed that some time in the night we would be within sight of land. Our course included passing through the San Bernardino Strait instead of north of the Batanes.

"Look," they said, giving way.

Through the porthole I saw land. I swallowed a lump in my throat.

"The land of the morning!" the lawyer declaimed.

I lay down again and put the blanket over my head.

The excitement on board was rather general, showing no signs of abatement as time went by.

On a warm afternoon as I stood in the shade, watching the green hills on every side, suddenly I saw the familiar outline of a mountain.

"Mount Mayon!" I cried, pointing to the shadow against the sky. And suddenly I thought of home, the nipa house at the foot of the volcano, my loved ones who had suffered and were now waiting for me after the wasted years. And I thought of those who were no longer there, Greg and Leling and Dodoy. Mother, too—thin brown arms and a sad voice, the smell of betel nut in her breath; the scent of lime in her hair.

"That's Mount Mayon, isn't it?" someone asked.

I turned to see a priest standing beside me.

"Yes, Father," I said, trying to smile, "that's where I live, at the foot of Mount Mayon."

"I see," he said, looking away in kindness.

He was Father Ocampo. He and his companion priests were in Rome when Hitler's soldiers started marching all over Europe. But these priests managed to take passage later on one of the exchange ships that plied between Europe and America. The three of them finished their doctorate in the United States.

Then I told him about myself. Before I knew it, I was confiding a lot of things to him. So we walked up and down the deck as he listened in silence and deep understanding. Before I knew it, I had confessed to him.

The next morning, I heard mass. The altar was a ping-pong table in the recreation room. One of the Filipino officers, a captain in the infantry, assisted in the mass. It was an early mass, but the recreation room was almost full. Father Ocampo gave a brief sermon.

He said, "By tomorrow, we shall be on Philippine soil again. Those of us who are coming home for the first time in many years will be shocked to see the ruins of our towns and cities. We are prepared for such sights. We have seen pictures of our blasted cities. But there are ruins other than the eyes can see. Men whose spirits the war had scarred, men who had seen the worst, known the darkest things, whose faith the war has shaken or completely destroyed. It might not be easy for those of us whom the war had not touched, who had not lived in a captured country, or known fear and despair, to understand what it is to live among embittered men. If you find nothing but indifference where you expected kindness, suspicion instead of trust; or find the dearest ideals which you have cherished all this time as scarce or completely gone as the goodness you believed reposed in most men, pray, my friends, that such things do not last for long."

As he spoke the sun came up from the sea. From the nearby land floated the scent of leaves and other growing things. Later, as I raised my head, after communion, I now could tell their names. I saw woodland and bare sloping hillocks, but no ruins. The ruins appeared later.

As we went through the pier, we saw the twisted steel and the powdered stones, the charred remains of what used to be Manila's skyline.

Pablo scanned the faces of the people crowding at the pier, but he turned away, unable this time to play his little game of make-believe. We looked over the heads of the people at the battered walls beyond, but we could not miss seeing the frantic hands waving welcome, the embraces, the tears. Pablo passed a trembling hand over his face as he paused on the landing. Then I saw an old man embrace Father Ocampo.

How indeed, Father, rebuild the other ruins? Could old men do it by dying in a land they had decided to call their own? Or was it done by scattering toys all over the land, rattlers and kiddie cars, balloons and electric trains, guns, grimacing clowns and dolls with upswept lashes, that childhood might start with laughter and kindness? Or would it help if the dumb were made to speak at last and the deaf hear and understand? Or would songs do it; wisdom perhaps? Or, maybe, prayer? There is a way, but it could not be the way of trembling hands with so many things to hide, nor could it be the way of that woman, holding a fatherless child in her arm, dragging a duffle bag by her side, now walking slowly toward the ruins of the city.

## LETTER: THE FARAWAY SUMMER

*Bob, I hope you're right, but I'm not so sure. It might not be easy* any more for me to get a passport back to Washington, D.C., unless you can fix it up with my boss, you know him, I hope he still has some use for a fellow like me. He might write to somebody at the Embassy. He used to ask me, are you sure, Pablo, you want to go home now? At this time? You might not have easy sailing back home in the Philippines, Pablo. Nothing but ruins there. Think it over.

Well, I thought it over and decided to come home anyhow.

But I got the bad breaks, that's all. Tell him, tell him everything, he will understand. And he knows you well, Bob. He had seen you often with me. How's your family, how's Rose? Your girl sure could cook. Tell her I often get hungry here just thinking of the broiled mackerel and lemon she used to fix for us. You're lucky, Bob. Me, I got the bad breaks.

You heard of the typhoon. Left me flat broke. I had everything invested on my farm. Now everything is gone, the crops, the tractor, my house, everything. I can't do nothing here. Been doing nothing at all these past months, just twiddling my thumbs, trying to make up my mind whether to stay and try again or go back to old Mr. Williams in Washington. Fix it up with him, will you? I can sell my land, but just now nobody's buying. But I'll manage, I'm willing to start all over again. Or is there someone working permanently for Mr. Williams now? But try. The old man liked me.

Yes, I've been to Manila. I remembered Steve. Of course,

you do. Steve the doctor. Remember now? Every time you
called him Doc, he'd get sore and say, just call me Steve. Boy,
how long ago was that? How's the housing condition there
now? It was terrific in those days. I had that little cottage on
the outskirts of the district near Silver Springs. Say, who's
staying there now? Steve was kind of wandering that summer,
not knowing where to live so I gave him the extra room. Boy,
he turned it into something special, didn't he, though? Oh, we
had fun, me cooking for him, and you and Rose and some of
the boys coming around Saturday nights, and Doc would be
taking the blood pressure of the fat ones and their drink-sotted
girls, and he'd be telling us lots of things about the Philippines. He looked funny with that embroidered apron around
him, as he dried the dishes. He was real good. When the war
broke out, he joined, he had to, being a doctor, and it broke
my heart to see him go. And I couldn't go with him. The army
didn't want an old man with trembling hands.

You'd remember Steve. He was nice looking in his uniform.
The first time he got a furlough, he comes up to my house and
says he had only a few hours left and he wanted fun. He
carried a big bundle of groceries and I called you up and you
came in your car. It was winter, by golly, how deep the snow
was, but you came to celebrate with us. And you remember,
of course, how it ended. That was funny. I wonder if you ever
told Rose about it.

I remember it all now, the three of us in the Chevvy, driving
through the snow just to get him to a house where he could
blow his money and his guts on some dame, he said it was his
last fling. And we let him. We stayed in the car and drove
around and waited and waited. We got numb with the cold.
We tried jumping up and down, cracking jokes, but no good.
The cold was getting us, but we couldn't leave him, didn't he
say it might be the last fling in his life? After a long time, he
came out, and there we were sneezing, quite numb all over,
but we were not sore. Don't worry, he said, I'll send you a
prescription if the cold gets worse. Well, we said goodbye and
he sent us cards from overseas. We followed him in our
minds, through London, through the fog and the blitz, and
how it was on D-Day, boy, the card we got from him was like

good-bye forever. Pray for me, he wrote, and we prayed as we knew how. We prayed sitting in my room with whiskey bottles and stuff all around. I guess we didn't really pray, we just sat there, thinking, thinking, till the tears stood in our eyes.

And that summer he got back, we were all in a fix. Who would tell him, how could we tell him that his entire family got wiped out during liberation in Manila, and that I was keeping many letters for him from an only surviving sister? He was so gay. The war was over. He was going home. Well, that night I left all the letters on his bed and waited for him. I saw him come, I saw him through the door, how he put the bed lamp on and saw the letters. How he tore them open. Then he knew. He flung himself on bed and no sound came from him. And he read on. Then he was crying. I had to close my door. You see a man cry and it isn't right. Something's real wrong. The next day we got drunk together, that is, he got drunk and I helped him home. Then he was all right. He'd stay in my room and talk about his folks as though they were still in the country waiting for him, as though he had never fought a war, as though there had been no war, no terrible things, just peace everywhere. Christmas-like, you know.

Well, after the typhoon, I came to Manila and looked for Steve. Maybe he could help me decide whether to stay and if I stayed, could he help me get a job, or if he said I could go back to the States, could he help me get a visa? It was not hard looking for him. But, boy, you should have seen Doc, his room was filled. Patients. What patients, not a single one of them looked sick, the room smelled more of perfume than medicine, I guess it's the same thing. His patients were the beautiful people of Manila, and I didn't feel so good sitting there, like I suddenly got nuts and sat among the guests of Mr. Williams in my work clothes, that's how I felt.

And when the nurse smiled at me to ask whether I wanted anything, I said, I wanted to see Steve. Steve? she asks, and I corrected myself and this nurse looks me up and down, I was shabby, you see the typhoon wet everything I had and I had nothing much except woolens I could not wear any more, besides, I liked khaki, but this nurse, she didn't seem to like it or it's my face maybe. Is it personal, she asks. You bet it is, I said, and I tell her if Steve is busy, I'd wait. So I waited and the patients came in and out of his room, and once I saw Steve push open the door for a fat dame, and I jumped. I was so excited to see him again, but he didn't see me, and I calmed down. He's very good looking now, he has put on weight, too.

I waited long, but it was comfortable waiting. You don't catch cold waiting in a room like that. Finally there were no more patients and Steve came out and told the nurse, well, that seems to be all for the day, and then he saw me. Oh, he said, thinking perhaps I was another patient. Then I came over to him. I couldn't keep calm any more. O boy, O boy, Steve, I said, and he looks surprised, at first I thought he didn't recognize me, but he did, and he grasped my hand, and I think he would have embraced me if there had been no girl around looking at us.

He pulled me with him to his room, come on in, come on in, he says. How long have you been waiting there, how are you, you aren't sick, I hope? You don't look sick.

Sick? I said, I'm strong as a carabao.

Good, he said laughing, and for some time we sat there looking at each other. He looked different. Maybe I looked different, too.

Then, he said, why . . . what . . . can I do for you?

He seemed serious suddenly, or kind of ashamed. Something must have gone wrong somewhere, a door had closed perhaps that should have remained open, or a window opened, that should have remained shut, I don't know, but suddenly, I knew something was not right.

So I told him my trouble about wanting to go back to the States, could he help me? He thought the matter over for a while, then he asked, in what way can I help you? So I hurried to explain that all I wanted was permission from the right people to go back to America. You should know some of the guys in the foreign office or in the American Embassy, I told him. Oh, sure, he said. So, when shall I see you again, I asked him. Come back, Wednesday, he said (it was Saturday then), but don't come during my consultation hours. I'm sorry, I said, I didn't know these things. Four o'clock, Wednesday, he said. Then he stood up, meaning I got to blow. So I prepared to go, not knowing what to say.

As I was going through the swinging door, he called. He didn't say, Pablo, he just said, Hey! like I was a stranger, suppose I just write you a letter, you don't have to come back, save you time, please give your name and address to the lady out there, and the last glimpse I had of him, he was picking up the phone.

The nurse picked up a pen and paper and waited as I stood in front of her. Pablo Icarañgal, I said. How do you spell that, she asks. Now Steve was dialing the phone. And thoughts kept coming to me. There was a phone, too, in my cottage, I recalled. His voice had not changed, now he was talking: Darling, I should have called earlier, but I just got rid of a visitor . . . no, no it wasn't a girl . . . a man, a Pinoy . . . I said *Pinoy* just one of those *Pinoys* I had met in the States . . .

Forget it sister, I said, leaving the doctor's clinic.

So you see, Bob, I'm not sure I'll get a visa. You got to fix it up with Mr. Williams. Meanwhile I could look around for a job, but I doubt if I'll get one. I'm not quite impressive looking, you know, besides, I'm too old now. Then I have no more friends here, really. Steve was one swell friend. Do you know what I felt like doing as soon as I left his clinic?

You see, out here, they got a custom among the rich. When a member of their family dies, the surviving members pay for an ad which says the guy is dead, how old he was, whom he left behind, and please to pray for his soul. I guess it works. So, I wanted to buy an ad in the papers which says, the friends of Dr. Esteban Hernandez, pray for his soul, he died today in his clinic while talking to a girl friend on the phone. He died without memories. Pray for his soul.

But that would be a crazy thing to do.

Well, you write me, Bob. Out here in this warm country, you do not remember the faraway summers. You do not remember period. I think it is better that way.

# THE DAY THE DANCERS CAME

*As soon as Fil woke up, he noticed a whiteness outside, quite un-*usual for the November mornings they had been having. That fall, Chicago was sandman's town, sleepy valley, drowsy gray, slumbrous mistiness from sunup till noon when the clouds drifted away in cauliflower clusters and suddenly it was evening. The lights shone on the avenues like soiled lamps centuries old and the skyscrapers became monsters with a thousand sore eyes. Now there was a brightness in the air and Fil knew what it was and he shouted, "Snow! It's snowing!"

Tony, who slept in the adjoining room, was awakened.

"What's that?" he asked.

"It's snowing," Fil said, smiling to himself as if he had ordered this and was satisfied with the prompt delivery. "Oh, they'll love this, they'll love this."

"Who'll love that?" Tony asked, his voice raised in annoyance.

"The dancers, of course," Fil answered. "They're arriving today. Maybe they've already arrived. They'll walk in the snow and love it. Their first snow, I'm sure."

"How do you know it wasn't snowing in New York while they were there?" Tony asked.

"Snow in New York in early November?" Fil said. "Are you crazy?"

"Who's crazy?" Tony replied. "Ever since you heard of those dancers from the Philippines, you've been acting nuts. Loco. As if they're coming here just for you."

113

Tony chuckled. Hearing him, Fil blushed, realizing that he had, indeed, been acting too eager, but Tony had said it. It felt that way—as if the dancers were coming here only for him.

Filemon Acayan, Filipino, was fifty, a U.S. citizen. He was a corporal in the U.S. Army, training at San Luis Obispo, on the day he was discharged honorably, in 1945. A few months later, he got his citizenship papers. Thousands of them, smart and small in their uniforms, stood at attention in drill formation, in the scalding sun, and pledged allegiance to the flag and the republic for which it stands. Soon after he got back to work. To a new citizen, work meant many places and many ways: factories and hotels, waiter and cook. A timeless drifting; once he tended a rose garden and took care of a hundred-year-old veteran of a border war. As a menial in a hospital in Cook County, all day he handled filth and gore. He came home smelling of surgical soap and disinfectant. In the hospital, he took charge of a row of bottles on a shelf, each bottle containing a stage of the human embryo in preservatives, from the lizard-like fetus of a few days, through the newly born infant, with its position unchanged, cold and cowering and afraid. He had nightmares through the years of himself inside a bottle. That was long ago. Now he had a more pleasant job as special policeman in the post office.

He was a few years younger than Tony—Antonio Bataller, a retired Pullman porter—but he looked older in spite of the fact that Tony had been bedridden most of the time for the last two years, suffering from a kind of wasting disease that had frustrated doctors. All over Tony's body, a gradual peeling was taking place. At first, he thought it was merely *tinia flava*, a skin disease common among adolescents in the Philippines. It had started around the neck and had spread to his extremities. His face looked as if it was healing from severe burns. Nevertheless, it was a young face, much younger than Fil's, which had never looked young.

"I'm becoming a white man," Tony had said once, chuckling softly.

It was the same chuckle Fil seemed to have heard now, only this time it sounded derisive, insulting.

Fil said, "I know who's nuts. It's the sick guy with the sick thoughts. You don't care for nothing but your pain, your imaginary pain."

"You're the imagining fellow. I got the real thing," Tony shouted from the room. He believed he had something worse than the whiteness spreading on his skin. There was a pain in his insides, like dull scissors scraping his intestines. Angrily, he added, "What for I got retired?"

"You're old, man, old, that's what, and sick, yes, but not cancer," Fil said turning towards the snow-filled sky. He pressed his face against the glass window. There's about an inch now on the ground, he thought, maybe more.

Tony came out of his room looking as if he had not slept all night. "I know what I got," he said, as if it were an honor and a privilege to die of cancer and Fil was trying to deprive him of it. "Never a pain like this. One day, I'm just gonna die."

"Naturally. Who says you won't?" Fil argued, thinking how wonderful it would be if he could join the company of dancers from the Philippines, show them around, walk with them in the snow, watch their eyes as they stared about them, answer their questions, tell them everything they wanted to know about the changing seasons in this strange land. They would pick up fistfuls of snow, crunch it in their fingers or shove it into their mouths. He had done just that the first time, long, long ago, and it had reminded him of the grated ice the Chinese sold near the town plaza where he had played *tatching* with an older brother who later drowned in a squall. How his mother had grieved over that death, she who had not cried too much when his father died, a broken man. Now they were all gone, quick death after a storm, or lingeringly, in a season of drought, all, all of them he had loved.

He continued, "All of us will die. One day. A medium bomb marked Chicago and this whole dump is *tapus*, finished. Who'll escape then?"

"Maybe your dancers will," Tony answered, now watching the snow himself.

"Of course, they will," Fil retorted, his voice sounding like a big assurance that all the dancers would be safe in his care. "The bombs won't be falling on this night. And, when the dancers are back in the Philippines . . ."

He paused, as if he was no longer sure of what he was going to say. "But maybe, even in the Philippines the bombs gonna fall, no?" he said, gazing sadly at the falling snow.

"What's that to you?" Tony replied. "You got no more folks ove'der, right? I know it's nothing to me. I'll be dead before that."

"Let's talk about something nice," Fil said, the sadness spreading on his face as he tried to smile. "Tell me, how will I talk, how am I gonna introduce myself?"

He would go ahead with his plans, introduce himself to the dancers and volunteer to take them sight-seeing. His car was clean and ready for his guests. He had soaped the ashtrays, dusted off the floor boards and thrown away the old mats, replacing them with new plastic throw rugs. He had got himself soaking wet while spraying the car, humming, as he worked, faintly remembered tunes from the old country.

Fil shook his head as he waited for Tony to say something. "Gosh, I wish I had your looks, even with those white spots, then I could face everyone of them," he said, "but this mug."

"That's the important thing, your mug. It's your calling card. It says, Filipino. Countryman," Tony said.

"You're not fooling me, friend," Fil said. "This mug says, Ugly Filipino. It says, old-timer, *muchacho*. It says Pinoy, *bejo*."

For Fil, time was the villain. In the beginning, the words he often heard were: too young, too young; but all of a sudden, too young became too old, too late. What had happened in between? A weariness, a mist covering all things. You don't have to look at your face in a mirror to know that you are old, suddenly old, grown useless for a lot of things and too late for all the dreams you had wrapped up well against a day of need.

"It also says sucker," Tony said. "What for you want to invite them? Here? Aren't you ashamed of this hole?"

"It's not a palace, I know," Fil answered, "but who wants a palace when they can have the most delicious *adobo* here and the best stuffed chicken . . . yum . . . yum . . ."

Tony was angry. "Yum, yum, you're nuts," he said, "plain and simple loco. What for you want to spend? You've been living on loose change all your life and now on a treasury warrant so small and full of holes, still you want to spend for these dancing kids who don't know you and won't even send you a card afterwards."

"Never mind the cards," Fil answered. "Who wants cards? But don't you see, they'll be happy; and then, you know what? I'm going to keep their voices, their words and their singing and their laughter in my magic sound mirror."

He had a portable tape recorder and a stack of recordings, patiently labeled, songs and speeches. The songs were in English, but most of the speeches were in the dialect, debates between him and Tony. It was evident Tony was the better speaker of the two in English, but in the dialect, Fil showed greater mastery. His style, however, was florid, sentimental, poetic.

Without telling Tony, he had experimented on recording sounds, like the way a bed creaked, doors opening and closing, rain or sleet tapping on the window panes, footsteps through the corridor. He played all the sounds back and tried to recall how it was on the day or night the sounds had been recorded. Did they bring back the moment? He was beginning to think that they did. He was learning to identify each of the sounds with a particular mood or fact. Sometimes, like today, he wished that there was a way of keeping a record of silence because it was to him the richest sound, like snow falling. He wondered as he watched the snow blowing in the wind, what took care of that moment if memory didn't. Like time, memory was often a villain, a betrayer.

"Fall, snow, fall," he murmured and, turning to Tony, said, "As soon as they accept my invitation, I'll call you up. No, you don't have to do anything, but I'd want you to be here to meet them."

"I'm going out myself." Tony said. "And I don't know what time I'll be back." Then he added, "You're not working today. Are you on leave?"

"For two days. While the dancers are here," Fil said.

"It still don't make sense to me," Tony said. "But good luck, anyway."

"Aren't you going to see them tonight? Our reserved seats are right out in front, you know."

"I know. But I'm not sure I can come."

"What? You're not sure?"

Fil could not believe it. Tony was indifferent. Something must be wrong with him. He looked at him closely, saying nothing.

"I want to, but I'm sick, Fil. I tell you, I'm not feeling so good. My doctor will know today. He'll tell me," Tony said.

"What will he tell you?"

"How do I know?"

"I mean, what's he trying to find out?"

"If it's cancer," Tony said. Without saying another word, he went straight back to his room.

Fil remembered those times, at night, when Tony kept him awake with his moaning. When he called out to him, asking, "Tony, what's the matter?" his sighs ceased for a while, but afterwards, Tony screamed, deadening his cries with a pillow agaist his mouth. When Fil rushed to his side, Tony drove him away. Or he curled up in the bedsheets like a big infant suddenly hushed in its crying. The next day, he would look all right. When Fil asked him about the previous night, he would reply, "I was dying," but it sounded more like disgust over a nameless annoyance.

Fil had misgivings, too, about the whiteness spreading on Tony's skin. He had heard of leprosy. Every time he thought of that dreaded disease, he felt tears in his eyes. In all the years he had been in America, he had not had a friend until he met Tony whom he liked immediately and, in a way, worshipped, for all the things the man had which Fil knew he himself lacked.

They had shared a lot together. They made merry on Christmas, sometimes got drunk and became loud. Fil recited poems in the dialect and praised himself. Tony fell to giggling and cursed all the railroad companies of America. But last Christmas, they hadn't gotten drunk. They hadn't even talked to each other on Christmas day. Soon, it would be Christmas again.

The snow was still falling.

"Well, I'll be seeing you," Fil said, getting ready to leave. "Try to be home on time. I shall invite the dancers for luncheon or dinner maybe, tomorrow. But tonight, let's go to the theater together, ha?"

"I'll try," Tony answered, adding after a pause, "Oh, Fil, I can't find my boots. May I wear yours?" His voice sounded strong and healthy.

"Sure, sure!" Fil answered. He didn't need boots. He loved to walk in the snow.

The air outside felt good. Fil lifted his face to the sky and closed his eyes as the snow and a wet wind drenched his face. He stood that way for some time, crying, more, more! to himself, drunk with snow and coolness. His car was parked a block away. As he walked towards it, he plowed into the snow with one foot and studied the scar he made, a hideous shape among perfect footmarks. He felt strong as his lungs filled with the cold air, as if just now it did not matter too much that he was the way he looked and his English the way it was. But perhaps, he could talk to the dancers in his dialect. Why not?

A heavy frosting of snow covered his car and as he wiped it off with his bare hands, he felt light and young, like a child at play, and once again, he raised his face to the sky and licked the flakes, cold and tasteless on his tongue.

When Fil arrived at the Hamilton, it seemed to him the Philippine dancers had taken over the hotel. They were all over the lobby on the mezzanine, talking in groups animatedly, their teeth sparkling as they laughed, their eyes disappearing in mere slits of light. Some of the girls wore their black hair long. For a moment, the sight seemed too much for him who had all but forgotten how beautiful Philippine girls were. He wanted to look away, but their loveliness held him. He must do something, close his eyes perhaps. As he did so, their laughter came to him like a breeze murmurous with sounds native to his land.

Later, he tried to relax, to appear inconspicuous. True, they were all very young, but there were a few elderly men and women who must have been their chaperons or well-wishers like him. He would smile at everyone who happened to look his way. Most of them smiled back, or rather, seemed to smile, but it was quick, without recognition, and might not have been for him but for someone else near or behind him.

His lips formed the words he was trying to phrase in his mind: *Ilocano ka? Bicol? Ano na, paisano? Comusta?* Or should he introduce himself? How? For what he wanted to say, the words didn't come too easily, they were unfamiliar, they stumbled and broke on his lips into a jumble of incoherence.

Suddenly, he felt as if he was in the center of a group where he was not welcome. All the things he had been trying to hide now showed: the age in his face, his horny hands. He knew it the instant he wanted to shake hands with the first boy who had drawn close to him, smiling and friendly. Fil put his hands in his pocket.

Now he wished Tony had been with him. Tony would know what to do. He would charm these young people with his smile and his learned words. Fil wanted to leave, but he seemed caught up in the tangle of moving bodies that merged and broke in a fluid strangle hold. Everybody was talking, mostly in English. Once in a while he heard exclamations in the dialect right out of the past, conjuring up playtime, long shadows of evening on the plaza, barrio fiestas, *misa de gallo*.

Time was passing and he had yet to talk to someone. Suppose he stood on a chair and addressed them in the manner of his flamboyant speeches recorded in his magic sound mirror?

"Beloved countrymen, lovely children of the Pearl of the Orient Seas, listen to me. I'm Fil Acayan. I've come to volunteer my services. I'm yours to command. Your servant. Tell me where you wish to go, what you want to see in Chicago. I know every foot of the lakeshore drive, all the gardens and the parks, the museums, the huge department stores, the planetarium. Let me be your guide. That's what I'm offering you, a free tour of Chicago, and finally, dinner at my apartment on West Sheridan Road—pork *adobo* and chicken *relleno*, name your dish. How about it, *paisanos?*"

No. That would be a foolish thing to do. They would laugh at him. He felt a dryness in his throat. He was sweating. As he wiped his face with a handkerchief, he bumped against a slim, short girl who quite gracefully stepped aside, and for a moment he thought he would swoon in the perfume that enveloped him. It was fragrance long forgotten, essence of *camia*, of *ilang-ilang*, and *dama de noche*.

Two boys with sleek, pomaded hair were sitting near an empty chair. He sat down and said in the dialect, "May I invite you to my apartment?" The boys stood up, saying, "Excuse us, please," and walked away. He mopped his brow, but instead of getting discouraged, he grew bolder as though he had moved one step beyond shame. Approaching another group, he repeated his invitation, and a girl with a mole on her upper lip, said, "Thank you, but we have no time." As he turned towards another group, he felt their eyes on his back. Another boy drifted towards him, but as soon as he began to speak, the boy said, "Pardon, please," and moved away.

They were always moving away. As if by common consent, they had decided to avoid him, ignore his presence. Perhaps it was not their fault. They must have been instructed to do so. Or was it his looks that kept them away? The thought was a sharpness inside him.

After a while, as he wandered about the mezzanine, among the dancers, but alone, he noticed that they had begun to leave. Some had crowded noisily into the two elevators. He followed the others going down the stairs. Through the glass doors, he saw them getting into a bus parked beside the subway entrance on Dearborn.

The snow had stopped falling; it was melting fast in the sun and turning into slush.

As he moved about aimlessly, he felt someone touch him on the sleeve. It was one of the dancers, a mere boy, tall and thin, who was saying, "Excuse, please." Fil realized he was in the way between another boy with a camera and a group posing in front of the hotel.

"Sorry," Fil said, jumping away awkwardly.

The crowd burst out laughing.

Then everything became a blur in his eyes, a moving picture out of focus, but gradually the figures cleared, there was mud on the pavement on which the dancers stood posing, and the sun threw shadows at their feet.

Let them have fun, he said to himself, they're young and

away from home. I have no business messing up their sched-
ule, forcing my company on them.

He watched the dancers till the last of them was on the bus.
The voices came to him, above the traffic sounds. They waved
their hands and smiled towards him as the bus started. Fil
raised his hand to wave back, but stopped quickly, aborting
the gesture. He turned to look behind him at whomever the
dancers were waving their hands to. There was no one there
except his own reflection in the glass door, a double exposure
of himself and a giant plant with its thorny branches around
him like arms in a loving embrace.


Even before he opened the door to their apartment, Fil knew
that Tony had not yet arrived. There were no boots outside on
the landing. Somehow he felt relieved, for until then he did
not know how he was going to explain his failure.

From the hotel, he had driven around, cruised by the lakeshore drive, hoping he would see the dancers somewhere, in a
park perhaps, taking pictures of the mist over the lake and the
last gold on the trees now wet with melted snow, or on some
picnic grounds, near a bubbling fountain. Still taking pictures
of themselves against a background of Chicago's gray and
dirty skyscrapers. He slowed down every time he saw a
crowd, but the dancers were nowhere along his way. Perhaps
they had gone to the theater to rehearse. He turned back before reaching Evanston.

He felt weak, not hungry. Just the same, he ate, warming up
some left-over food. The rice was cold, but the soup was hot
and tasty. While he ate, he listened for footfalls.

Afterwards, he lay down on the sofa and a weariness came
over him, but he tried hard not to sleep. As he stared at the
ceiling, he felt like floating away, but he kept his eyes open,
willing himself hard to remain awake. He wanted to explain
everything to Tony when he arrived. But soon his eyes closed
against a weary will too tired and weak to fight back sleep—
and then there were voices. Tony was in the room, eager to tell
his own bit of news.

"I've discovered a new way of keeping afloat," he was saying.

"Who wants to keep afloat?" Fil asked.

"Just in case. In a shipwreck, for example," Tony said.

"Never mind shipwrecks. I must tell you about the dancers," Fil said.

"But this is important," Tony insisted. "This way, you can keep floating indefinitely."

"What for indefinitely?" Fil asked.

"Say in a ship . . . I mean, in an emergency, you're stranded without help in the middle of the Pacific or the Atlantic, you must keep floating till help comes . . ." Tony explained.

"More better," Fil said, "find a way to reach shore before the sharks smells you. You discover that."

"I will," Tony said, without eagerness, as though certain that there was no such way, that, after all, his discovery was worthless.

"Now you listen to me," Fil said, sitting up abruptly. As he talked in the dialect, Tony listened with increasing apathy.

"There they were." Fil began, his tone taking on the orator's pitch, "who could have been my children if I had not left home—or yours, Tony. They gazed around them with wonder, smiling at me, answering my questions, but grudgingly, edging away as if to be near me were wrong, a violation in their rule book. But it could be that every time I opened my mouth, I gave myself away. I talked in the dialect, Ilocano, Tagalog, Bicol, but no one listened. They avoided me. They had been briefed too well: Do not talk to strangers. Ignore their invitations. Be extra careful in the big cities like New York and Chicago, beware of the old-timers, the Pinoys. Most of them are bums. Keep away from them. Be on the safe side—stick together, entertain only those who have been introduced to you properly.

"I'm sure they had such instructions, safety measures, they must have called them. What then could I have done, scream out my good intentions, prove my harmlessness and my love for them by beating my breast? Oh, but I loved them. You see,

I was like them once. I, too, was nimble with my feet, graceful with my hands; and I had the tongue of a poet. Ask the village girls and the envious boys from the city—but first you have to find them. After these many years, it won't be easy. You'll have to search every suffering face in the village gloom for a hint of youth and beauty or go where the graveyards are and the tombs under the lime trees. One such face . . . oh, God, what am I saying?

"All I wanted was to talk to them, guide them around Chicago, spend money on them so that they would have something special to remember about us here when they return to our country. They would tell their folks: We met a kind, old man, who took us to his apartment. It was not much of a place. It was old—like him. When we sat on the sofa in the living room, the bottom sank heavily, the broken springs touching the floor. But what a cook that man was! And how kind! We never thought that rice and *adobo* could be that delicious. And the chicken *relleno!* When someone asked what the stuffing was—we had never tasted anything like it—he smiled saying, 'From heaven's supermarket,' touching his head and pressing his heart like a clown as if heaven were there. He had his tape recorder which he called a magic sound mirror, and he had all of us record our voices. Say anything in the dialect, sing, if you please, our *kundiman,* please, he said, his eyes pleading, too. Oh, we had fun listening to the playback. When you're gone, the old man said, I shall listen to your voices with my eyes closed and you'll be here again and I won't ever be alone, no, not anymore, after this. We wanted to cry, but he looked very funny, so we laughed and he laughed with us.

"But, Tony, they would not come. They thanked me, but they said they had no time. Others said nothing. They looked through me. I didn't exist. Or worse, I was unclean. *Basura.* Garbage. They were ashamed of me. How could I be Filipino?"

The memory, distinctly recalled, was a rock on his breast. He gasped for breath.

"Now, let me teach you how to keep afloat," Tony said, but it was not Tony's voice.

Fil was alone and gasping for air. His eyes opened slowly till he began to breathe more easily. The sky outside was gray. He looked at his watch—a quarter past five. The show would begin at eight. There was time. Perhaps Tony would be home soon.

The apartment was warming up. The radiators sounded full of scampering rats. He had a recording of that in his sound mirror.

Fil smiled. He had an idea. He would take the sound mirror to the theater, take his seat close to the stage, and make tape recordings of the singing and the dances.

Now he was wide-awake and somehow pleased with himself. The more he thought of the idea, the better he felt. If Tony showed up now . . . He sat up, listening. The radiators were quiet. There were no footfalls, no sound of a key turning.

Late that night, back from the theater, Fil knew at once that Tony was back. The boots were outside the door. He, too, must be tired, and should not be disturbed.

He was careful not to make any noise. As he turned on the floor lamp, he thought that perhaps Tony was awake and waiting for him. They would listen together to a playback of the dances and the songs Tony had missed. Then he would tell Tony what happened that day, repeating part of the dream.

From Tony's bedroom came the regular breathing of a man sound alseep. To be sure, he looked into the room and in the half-darkness, Tony's head showed darkly, deep in a pillow, on its side, his knees bent, almost touching the clasped hands under his chin, an oversized fetus in the last bottle. Fil shut the door between them and went over to the portable. Now. He turned it on to low. At first nothing but static and odd sounds came through, but soon after there was the patter of feet to the rhythm of a familiar melody.

All the beautiful boys and girls were in the room now, dancing and singing. A boy and a girl sat on the floor holding two bamboo poles by their ends flat on the floor, clapping them together, then apart, and pounding them on the boards, while dancers swayed and balanced their lithe forms, dipping their bare brown legs in and out of the clapping bamboos, the pace gradually increasing into a fury of wood on wood in a counterpoint of panic among the dancers and in a harmonious flurry of toes and ankles escaping certain pain—crushed bones, and bruised flesh, and humiliation. Other dances followed, accompanied by songs and live with the sounds of life and death in the old country; Igorot natives in G-strings walking down a mountainside; peasants climbing up a hill on a rainy day; neighbors moving a house, their sturdy legs showing under a moving roof; lovers at Lent hiding their passion among wild hedges, far from the crowded chapel; a distant gong sounding off a summons either to a feast or a wake. And finally, prolonged ovation, thunderous, wave upon wave . . .

"Turn that thing off!" Tony's voice was sharp above the echoes of the gongs and the applause settling into silence.

Fil switched off the dial and in the sudden stillness, the voices turned into faces, familiar and near, like gesture and touch that stayed on even as the memory withdrew, bowing out, as it were, in a graceful exit, saying, thank you, thank you, before a ghostly audience that clapped hands in silence and stomped their feet in a sucking emptiness. He wanted to join the finale, such as it was, pretend that the curtain call included him, and attempt a shamefaced imitation of a graceful adieu, but he was stiff and old, incapable of grace; but he said, thank you, thank you, his voice sincere and contrite, grateful for the other voices and the sound of singing and the memory.

"Oh, my God . . ." the man in the other room cried, followed by a moan of such anguish that Fil fell on his knees, covering the sound mirror with his hands to muffle the sounds that had started again, it seemed to him, even after he had turned it off.

Then he remembered.

"Tony, what did the doctor say? What did he say?" he shouted and listened, holding his breath, no longer able to tell at the moment who had truly waited all day for the final sentence.

There was no answer. Meanwhile, under his hands, there was a flutter of wings, a shudder of gongs. What was Tony saying? That was his voice, no? Fil wanted to hear, he must know. He switched dials on and off, again and again, pressing buttons. Suddenly, he didn't know what to do. The spools were live, they kept turning. His arms went around the machine, his chest pressing down on the spools. In the quick silence, Tony's voice came clear.

"So they didn't come after all?"

"Tony, what did the doctor say?" Fil asked, straining hard to hear.

"I knew they wouldn't come. But that's okay. The apartment is old anyhow. And it smells of death."

"How you talk. In this country, there's a cure for everything."

"I guess we can't complain. We had it good here all the time. Most of the time, anyway."

"I wish, though, they had come. I could . . ."

"Yes, they could have. They didn't have to see me, but I could have seen them. I have seen their pictures, but what do they really look like?"

"Tony, they're beautiful, all of them, but especially the girls. Their complexion, their grace, their eyes, they were what we call talking eyes, they say things to you. And the scent of them!"

There was a sigh from the room, soft, hardly like a sigh. A louder, grating sound, almost under his hands that had relaxed their hold, called his attention. The sound mirror had kept going, the tape was fast unravelling.

"Oh, no!" he screamed, noticing that somehow, he had pushed the eraser.

Frantically, he tried to rewind and play back the sounds and the music, but there was nothing now but the dull creaking of the tape on the spool and meaningless sounds that somehow had not been erased, the thud of dancing feet, a quick clapping of hands, alien voices and words: *in this country . . . everything . . . all of them . . . talking eyes . . . and the scent . . .* a fading away into nothingness, till about the end when there was a screaming, senseless kind of finale detached from the body of a song in the background, drums and sticks and the tolling of a bell.

"Tony! Tony!" Fil cried, looking towards the sick man's room, "I've lost them all."

Biting his lips, Fil turned towards the window, startled by the first light of dawn. He hadn't realized till then the long night was over.

# THE CONTENDER

*Bernie was sorry afterwards. He listened, unsmiling, to the foot-*falls on the corridor until they were echoes fading away in a whimper of other sounds in the building, an angry voice, a dirty word, a telephone ringing, ringing, and then a click, another voice, a closing door, radiators acting up like scamper-ing rats caught in a heated trap.

Winter came early that year in Chicago. The mild autumn had become increasingly violent, the trees shedding their leaves before they had turned deep gold. By October the flur-ries of wind raking the dead leaves on the twilight streets and parks bore the snow-dusts of winter. Now in November there was slush and ice on the avenues and the lake winds bit into the covered flesh like thrusts of pain into the naked body.

Felix had been nagging him to see a doctor about his eyes since that day during the last summer when, walking out of the post office, Bernie felt the darkness fall and everything around him became shadows. It was early afternoon and hot. He stopped to wipe his face. He closed his eyes and rubbed them gently with his fingers. When he opened them, the dark-ness was still there, a thin veil with shadows walking about in all directions. It did not last long, however, perhaps less than a minute, and then the veil was gone. He could see clearly again, the pressing of crowds and automobiles dragging by, the sun on the streets and the glare of signs. When he told Felix about it then, Felix had said, "You need an eye special-ist, man. You got to see one right away."

There had been other attacks since, short intervals of sudden evening. The worst happened the day the dancers came, right in the middle of the show. At first Bernie thought something had gone wrong with the lights on the stage. The darkness was total. He waited for the usual whistling and shouting, but instead the songs and the dances went on. Turning to the men around him, he couldn't see anyone. Everybody was strangely quiet. Then he knew. Another spell. But this was different, this was no thin veil with shadows, this was a blackout, complete and . . . final? Would the lights go on again for him? He swallowed hard, his hands going frantically to his eyes. Those around him should not notice. With his eyes still closed, he rubbed them gently. It was still pitch dark when he opened them. He shivered. It was chilly in the dark. He felt as if it were sucking him into an icy whirlpool. Meanwhile that music, those sounds of dancing feet, how sweet and familiar and happy. Thunderous applause. He, too, clapped his hands, weakly, even as he prayed, "Let me see again, God, oh, please, let me!"

It took a long time before he could see again. Yet nobody seemed to have noticed him. The stage appeared nearer and brighter. A lovely Philippine maiden walked proudly under a parasol held up by dusky slaves, and at the sound of a gong, she began to dance, swaying about in fluid grace, her arms and wrists and long-nailed fingertips sharpening the rhythm of her dance. Her eyes flashed like those of a warrior maiden wondering about love.

Bernie felt the salt of his tears on his lips, but he stared on and clapped his hands, louder this time as the house shook with a mighty ovation at the finale: the proud brown maid, no longer proud, crumpled in a heap of velvet and satin on the floor, knowing at last what love was because she missed it now.

Of course, he was going to see a doctor. There was no need for Felix to nag him the way he did. No need to hurry. Perhaps he didn't have to go after all. His eyes were perfect, otherwise. He didn't even need glasses. Things like these spells happened to old guys. He was already past sixty. He had been through a lot, his eyes had seen the strangest things. But he was going to see a doctor just the same. There was no sense quarreling the way they did, saying those nasty things that made him fighting mad.

"So you don't want to see a doctor, eh?" Felix was screaming at him. "You're just going to sit on your ass until you go stark blind and then I got to buy you pencils you can sell at the street corner, eh?"

"Leave me alone, will you?" Bernie shouted back. He had been afraid of that. No one need remind him. Not even Felix.

"Are you scared? Yellow?" Felix mocked.

"Who's scared? Look, who's yellow?" Bernie compressed his lips that bore the scars of many blows he had not seen coming his way.

Bernie Canlas was a boxer, flyweight, when Felix Magat, a plantation laborer like him in Hawaii, took over as manager and promoted his fights on the West Coast.

In his youth Bernie could hardly write his name; but he learned fast with all those contracts Felix kept asking him to sign. He taught himself how to read and write. Nothing to it. He and Felix were always together in those days. True, they had occasional quarrels, but this was different. There was no sense to it.

And no one had the right to call him yellow. Felix ought to know by now that Bernie was no coward. No, sir. Remember, Felix, that time you threw the towel in my fight with Kid Kelly in Frisco? Bernie listened. It was his own voice. All over the building a silence had settled that reminded him of angelus in the hometown on a cold evening.

It was in the seventh round. He didn't see the blow coming. No pain. Just blackness. When he came to, he was sitting on the stool in his corner and Felix was asking him, "You awright?"

"Sure, I'm awright." To prove it, he jumped up and began swinging.

Felix pulled him back to the stool. "Take it easy now," he said, uneasily. "You're lucky the bell saved you." Now it was ringing again.

Bernie rushed his opponent. Before the round was over, blood from many cuts was all over his face. He kept wiping it off his eyes. The crowd was howling for more blood. Then Felix threw the towel. Bernie ran to him, crying through the blood in his mouth, "I'm okay. I wanna fight some more. I'm okay, see?" He started shadow boxing, splattering everything and everybody around him with blood. Felix put a huge robe around Bernie and pulled him away.

"But why? why? I could have beat him!" Bernie cried as Felix led him through the crowd that had already forgotten him. The next fight had started.

Bernie Canlas had never won a championship. He never made anything better than runner-up. He was always contending for the championship. Second best. That was the most for him. The championship was either a step ahead or far away, practically out of sight. From runner-up, he took one disastrous defeat after another till he had to begin all over again from the bottom. After every loss, alone in the locker room, he went over every round up to the final blow. How come he was wide open and he didn't know? Something wrong with his reflexes, his eyes? He knew what the prize was, but most of the time it was beyond his reach no matter how hard he tried. When it seemed nearest, he was always there, picking himself up from the sodden canvas, the stinging tears on his wounds. Felix hustled as much as he could for his boxer friend, wondering what was happening to his boy. Bernie had shown so much promise in the beginning. This guy was different. He knew Bernie was washed-up, a has-been, long before Bernie himself realized it.

In his last fight, Bernie was knocked out on his feet. He just stood there taking in all the blows, but he never buckled under. Nothing to it. The fight, however, had to be stopped to save Bernie from further punishment.

"What's wrong with you?" Felix asked.

"Nothing's wrong with me. I just couldn't see 'em coming, that's what," Bernie answered, wiping his tears. He wept every time he lost. But he wept even more when occasionally, he won.

"You're washed-up," Felix told him.

"I know," he admitted, shaking his head.

Afterwards, Bernie tried odd jobs, but finally he learned

how to cut hair just like Felix who soon had a barbershop of his own. Together they went to the Midwest and settled in Chicago. They liked it there. Business was good. Bernie worked for his friend. Above the mirror in front of the barber's chair were framed clippings and pictures of the old days when Bernie was still Fighting Bernie, strongest contender for the Flyweight Championship of Central Luzon. Bernie in his favorite stance, gloved fists just over the chin, below the slanting eyes, the eyebrows thick with scars, only one cauliflower ear showing. Or his hands raised in victory, his mouth in a wide grin, matching Felix's, standing proud and tall beside him.

When Felix decided to return to the Philippines to get himself a wife, Bernie took over the barbershop and ran it well, sending as much money as Felix wanted now and then. In three months, Felix was back with a brown buxom woman, young enough to be his daughter, whom he had married. He had pictures of the wedding: the couple standing in front of a huge wedding cake, the girl shoving a spoonful into his open laughing mouth, long rows of tables full of grinning men and women.

Bernie wanted to do the same, return to the Philippines and get himself a wife, but he never got around to it. There was always an impediment: no money, no time, or just any old excuse—no guts perhaps.

To keep in trim, he walked a lot, he did his push-up exercises for as long as he could. When there was no one around in the barbershop, he did shadow-boxing, ran in circles, did bending exercises, or kept jabbing at the guy in the mirror. As the years came and went, he found his legs no longer responding well. Now he tired easily. Then his eyes began to fail. How could he continue being a barber? Did the customers complain to Felix? Did he notice? Perhaps he did.

"See a doc. Don't be too sure about your eyes," he kept telling Bernie.

But when Felix mentioned the pencils, Bernie really got mad.

"Leave me alone, will you?" he shouted. "I'm tired and sick of your nagging."

"You're nuts. Punch drunk, that's what you are. I'm only trying to help you."

"Who wants your help? Go away."

"Oh, now he's independent."

"Go away! Go away!" he screamed at Felix.

"All right, you can go to hell," Felix shouted, banging the door shut as he marched down the corridor to the flight of stairs at the far end.

Bernie was sorry as hell. No sense fighting the only pal he had. Besides, he was really going to see a doctor. But what could the doctor say? He was okay.

The eye specialist wore thick-rimmed glasses. He was not too tall, but he was a heavyweight, Bernie was sure about that. After the preliminary questions, he told Bernie to fill out a form. Easy. He could write very well and read better than some college guys he knew.

Then the doctor took him to a dark room, an air-conditioned cubicle with black curtains. He was made to sit on a cold steel chair. The doctor peered into his eyes with a small pin-prick of light that came from the tip of a silver pen he carried in his hand like a toy.

There were questions, instructions, and more questions, while the light probed into his eyes. The doctor sat so close, his body pressed against him, he could hear the doctor's breath and smell the peculiar body odor he had learned to associate with Americans.

"Your eyes are okay," the doctor said.

The words reassured him. Felix should hear that.

"Have you ever fought in the ring?" the doctor asked.

"Sure, I've fought in the ring," Bernie replied.

"That's it," the doctor said, switching on the light. He stared at the scarred face. Bernie wanted to hide it behind his hands. But even his hands . . .

"Your eyes are okay," the doctor didn't seem to know what else to say. He seemed too embarrassed to say otherwise. "Those blackout spells must be due to something else." He looked at the form Bernie had filled, and added, "I'll tell you what. Come back in a week, at the same time, okay? Take it easy now."

Bernie rang up Felix from the barbershop.

"I seen a doctor," he said as soon as he recognized his friend's voice.

"What did he say?" Felix asked as though there had been no fight earlier and the two were on the best of terms.

"He says my eyes are okay," Bernie told him.

"See another doctor," Felix said.

"Here we go again."

"How about having supper with us?"

Bernie made excuses. After his friend's marriage, Bernie stayed away as much as he could, although they met every day in the barbershop. When the couple had their first child, he was around to see it baptized. Now there were five in the family, all grown-ups, all going to school like prim rich ladies who drove their own cars. They said "Hi" when he met them. The truth was, he never felt at home with Felix's family.

Many times he found himself comparing his luck with Felix's, who got all the breaks. Compared to Felix, he was nothing now but a broken-down old man, slowly getting blind. There, the truth was out at last. He didn't have to go back to the hospital to know what the final decision would be: "Take it easy now. You're going blind. There's nothing that can be done about it."

Strange, it was not the future he thought of most of the time, but the past, as if now, at this point, there was still a way out, of correcting the slips that had passed unnoticed, redirecting forces and events, altering them or simply inventing excuses for acts that appeared senseless now and without motive. Everything that was past and behind wouldn't have happened: if I had not stayed away from home too long . . . if I had married . . . if I didn't have too much pride . . . if I had been alert enough to see the blows coming . . . if I had not been such a blasted fool.

There was a time when he could have passed for ten or fifteen years younger in spite of his mug, except for his hands that showed the many things he wanted to hide: ignorance of a sort in the midst of so much knowledge, a loneliness so overpowering it had color and sound and smell and a body that pressed against him like the touch of death.

Nobody would have him now. But even in those days when he was younger, the girls he wanted to marry married other guys no better than he, some of them worse, good for nothing, no account characters. Each girl tagged along until the other guy came along—as in the song—and took her away from him.

It was ever thus. The girls he had loved were always being taken away from him. Some, like Elsie Manning and Dorothy Clark were kind to him long afterwards. They never snubbed him even after they had men of their own. Not with Elaine Weeks, the tall one, taller than he (he spent all he earned on her, the bitch!) or Louise Bixler who was violent when drunk, or when sober, was gross. The names she had called him! And those others whose names he had forgotten.

So he stopped falling in love. He made dirty jokes about love which he called a four-letter word. He began dating girls for the hell of it when he wanted company, when being alone was a little too much to bear, particularly in spring when the parks were full or in summer when the girls wore such flimsy dresses they practically had no dresses at all. This worked out well until, not a few years back, he met Selma Goldman who sold recordings of the latest song hits in a department store. She was no longer young. About his age. Their affair lasted a long time, until shortly before his eyes began to fail him. Sometimes she visited him in his room. She knocked very gently as if she was not sure she wanted to see him. But mostly, he stayed with her in her apartment on the other side of the city. They used to make love, gently, but later, they didn't make love anymore. They just lay there in each other's arms in the dark, safe from voices and footsteps, feeling coolness and warmth, till sleep came. Even after a bath, Selma smelled the same sweet sourish kitchen smell of spices hoarded and forgotten. Afterwards, no matter what the time was, past midnight or before dawn, or the season of the year, she walked with him to the bus stop and as the bus left, they waved to each other as if it were the last time. Then one day, it was really the last time though neither knew it was.

The last visit to the doctor proved him right. Felix had insisted that he accompany him. On the way, Bernie kept saying, "This trip isn't necessary. I know what the doctor's gonna say."

"Don't be a fool," Felix said.

This time there were four doctors who examined him all over again. They were heavyweights, six-footers, too. And very kind. They said it wouldn't be too bad, really. For a long time there would be no complete blackout, just a kind of brownout. He would be able to see the outlines of objects, moving or still.

"Now, who's the fool?" Bernie said on their way from the hospital.

He had remained a boxer too long. He had wanted victory too much.

"I'll take you home. Or you stay with us," Felix said.

"I'd rather sell pencils," Bernie said.

Of course, he didn't have to. Social security (what a name!) would surely be a great help. Nothing to it. Just like going into the final round with a broken arm, eyes covered with blood. It was like sitting in his corner waiting for the bell. But all the bells had been taken away. The stadium was empty and all the lights had been doused. Under a steady flame, the water simmered. Soon all the silver things would be sterilized. The scented towels, too hot to touch, were ready. Easy. Close your eyes now. Bay rum and antiseptics filled the locker room. Locker room? Barbershop? There was an overlapping in the memory.

Shortly afterwards. Bernie had another attack. Somehow, even after the initial blackout, he could hardly see any more. Just what the doctor had said. He was ready. Felix was on hand to take him to his room.

"Don't worry about anything," Felix said.

"I don't see you too good, but you sound more worried than I," Bernie said.

"I'll see you as often as I can," Felix promised.

"Do that," Bernie said, very calm, and added, "Please send me those pictures and the clippings all framed up right over the mirror where my name plate is. You can have that, if you want it."

Felix left without another word.

Bernie listened to his footfalls.

Anyway, the darkness was a partial referee, always in his favor. In the dark, he could be anywhere. Besides, it was not total darkness. Whoever had decreed that the light be outlawed in his little island had consented to a compromise, a perpetual twilight. Of course, it was only a temporary truce. Yet when the true darkness finally settled, how would he know, how could he tell, when voices started talking to him, which was real? Hold out his hand? Learn to listen with his heart?

With the darkness there was a last gift, like leftover grace. Now he understood a lot of things that were not clear to him before. In the long night, the voices were not only clearer but kinder.

The knocking on the door was always gentle now like Selma's in the good old days before the end. One day perhaps they would all be here for a final leave-taking. Elsie and Dot, Elaine, Louise, and the nameless ones, Felix among them with his bag of groceries and his sad voice, the hairy apes he had contended with in the ring, perhaps, even God, why not? with another contract. He was ready and willing to sign any time. Nothing to it.

Meanwhile, thank God for this, at least, this little left before the end, a slow and gradual approach into the center of the final ring. Start of the last round. A hasty brush of gloves supposed to be a handshake. Crouch, crouch, dance to the beat of animal voices crying blood. A feint, a swish of leather, a flailing of hands. An embrace, an agony. God, keep me on my feet. Give strength to these dying arms. The dancing form before me has become a monster, a hairy ape with hunger in his eyes. A shattering blow on the jaw without pain, the lemon rind flying off in a bubble of blood and sweat. Stars and birdsong, but I'm still on my feet and there is a bell singing in my head. The stars cling and swirl in a hum of voices: you're washed-up, man. I know . . . I know. Forgive me, friends, my countrymen, forgive me . . .

In spring Felix came with a cane, a beautiful one, he said.

Bernie felt its texture with his fingers and tried to see what he could of its color and finish.

"Just arrived in today's mail. From the Philippines," Felix said.

"Thanks a lot," Bernie said, clasping the crook of the cane. "Now I can get rid of this umbrella, except on rainy days."

When it was time to go Bernie saw Felix to the door, using the cane for the first time.

"Thanks, friend," he said, turning away as soon as he heard the door shut and waited for the other visitors who also brought him gifts out of the night.

# QUICKER WITH ARROWS

*For both of them there would be no fumbling for lost dates, no*
turning over the pages of the calendar for the particular year,
the definite month and day, no searching the memory for
echoes that now belonged to the past. Always, when their
minds turned to the first day, their first day together, like this,
together alone and in love, there would be no crashing of cymbals and a thunderous beat of drums and trumpets blowing,
sudden and frightening, as it was on that day in summer, was
it two or three years ago? It did not matter. Crowded Washington was stifling in the heat, there was a war going on, oh,
yes, it had just begun, and lovers who had since long perished
yet lived and loved, the same war that had already ended in
Europe and would soon end all over the world after Hiroshima.

It was a late afternoon, but the sunlight lay glaring still over
the heads of the lugubrious figures on the wall of the upper
story of the brown building across the way from the *Bayou*,
where Val had lived in an apartment since his arrival from
New York. The scene had not altered through the changing
seasons and faces.

From the open window, the lovers watched a raucous
parade of negroes attired in many colors like characters in a
costume play, clowns without their masks, toreadors without
their *muletas*, or gypsies grown weary with lying. All marched
to the loud music, their black, oily faces shiny in the sun,
dark, wet spots showing under their arms.

140

What was it all about, the blaring music and the marching men and women with hard, unsmiling faces?

It could be that these paraders belonged to a sect or a cult professing a faith others denied, fighting for a cause so flimsy that the voice had to be loud acclaiming it, and these drums and trumpets could be a renewal of courage slowly dying. Or maybe, this was to mark a day of triumph or perhaps the anniversary of a loss—the lovers never knew; they did not truly care.

Now long afterwards, suddenly remembering, Fay asked, "Those colored folks that day, remember? What were they really up to, do you think?"

"Maybe they were celebrating for us," Val replied. Fay took up the banter in his voice, saying, "But they looked so serious, they should have been gay and laughing."

"Think so?"

"Of course, Val, unless, perhaps, you regret all this?" The lightness in her voice was gone.

"Now, don't be silly, I was only joking," he said, drawing her close to him, the dampness of her flesh, a welcome coolness on his own.

Ever since that first day two or three years ago, there had been desperate moments in his life, only he knew, but not even he quite frankly admitted, for which he hated and cursed himself, his wanting Fay so much, delighting in the things she said and did for him without any thought of getting anything in return, or just happily content with her presence in the apartment. But there were times when he wished she would forget and leave him because, well, it did not seem right, it was not right. He was all so confused, sometimes he felt he was going mad . . . what did it all mean? was it love? what was it, really, but why find out? Just go on and on till the time came for parting. He was going home and leaving all this behind him. Perhaps even his tenderness, his passion, was just that, a manner of saying, Fay, this cannot last forever. I must return to my country, I must leave you behind. My people won't understand, I don't understand, darling, I'm confused. Help me, help me, whoever you are who could help me . . . Hence, every embrace was a last embrace, every burning kiss, the searing end.

Among the Filipinos and their American friends in Washington, Valentin Rustia was the brown prince, always impeccably dressed, always smiling and kind. But Val's kindness was the kindness of the weak. He could not stand suffering in others and he gloated over his own as though self-pity were the ultimate ecstasy. Sometimes he talked tough. Once, he was heard to say that, at least for the duration of the war, there should be a moratorium on feeling, an off-limits sign for all hearts.

Just returned from New York City where he was studying before the outbreak of the war, Val had many friends both among the Americans and the Filipinos. He was often seen in dances escorting pretty, clean-looking American girls, and, now and then, the daughters of Filipinos prominent in the homeland, studying in New York or in New England, in exclusive colleges for women.

The youngest son of a wealthy landowner from Pampanga, Val was sent to America to prepare him to take over his father's place at the sugar central which his family practically owned. There had been rumors linking his name with that of the accomplished and lovely daughter of a wealthy Visayan family, distant relatives of his mother who was once herself a beauty from the Visayas.

But Val was free and did not seem to feel the burdens and inconveniences that the war was imposing on everyone in America. Soon after the declaration of war between the United States and Japan, however, his regular allowance from home was cut off. He took on jobs nobody back home would have thought him capable of doing, until he met a former American senator, who was the spokesman for the sugar block in the Philippines, and a friend of his father's. Without difficulty, the former senator got him a job with the Washington Office of War Information. The job was classified essential and Val did not have to get into a uniform. There had been times, though, when he did not relish the sinecure he had landed. He wanted to get into the army and fight, or get wounded maybe, or even die, why not, so many young men who had as much right to remain alive and whole were getting all maimed in mind and body, and dying. Nothing lasted, anyhow, even life, especially life, such as it was.

When he met Fay, he expected her to go out of his life, just like so many others before, without regret, even without memories. Fay Price had not yet finished high school when she left her home in Virginia to work in the wrapping department of Hecht and Company in Washington. She attended high school, graduating at the outbreak of the war. When they met, Fay worked nights as cashier in a government cafeteria on Constitution Avenue. She was such a simple girl, she would every now and then speak out her fears to Val, in their early days together, asking what sort of spell he had cast upon her. She had met other men, handsomer and taller, and, like her, white, and you are brown, she would say, and not so tall, and your eyes disappear when you smile, but I love you, Val. This must be love, this wanting to be near you all the time, this thinking of you all day and feeling famished and missing you something awful and all broken up inside me till I see you and I am in your arms again.

She had spoken about it to her friends who advised her to forget Val, the sooner the better, for he was going to bring nothing but sorrow to her life. But that was not true, Val had not brought sorrow to her life. She was happy with him. Now there was some sort of meaning to her life, instead of living one dreary day after another, without hope, without something real to hold on to, an anchor, or something that says to you early in the morning when you wake up, now this is another day, and there will be a smile in his eyes as you look into them, and his arms will be strong, and his touch so gentle, you will feel all weak and trembly and lost, but alive, yes, alive, and wishing to live on and on, for him, whom you have found, for him whom you love.

Fay was understanding. When Val didn't feel like talking, she kept quiet, doing whatever she felt like doing, reading perhaps, or tidying up his things, he was so messy with his belongings. When he felt like talking about things she could not understand, she pretended to be interested and listened on. Now Val was also a good listener. When she talked to him about her life, the poverty of it, a shiftless, good for nothing father, who, on a violent day, clubbed her mother to death, the terrible life in an orphanage, she saw tears in his eyes. Val felt truly and deeply about such things and wondered why they should happen to a lovely creature like Fay. Part of his sadness must have been due to the realization that there was such a gap in their lives.

For her part, Fay felt that Val needed someone like her, to talk to, to love. There were times when he looked so helpless. He was so lonesome for home, he looked so radiant talking to her about his country and his folks, his beautiful mother, and his wealthy father, and the vast stretches of sugar cane fields, and the men at work, the private railways leading to the fields and the mills, how the cars were loaded with cane and the children of the tenants would pull at them as the box-cars passed their shacks; the Pampanga river, swollen and dark during the months of rain, the festivals, Easter and Christmas. During Easter, the fish was cooked in eggs, all eggs, you could hardly find the fish. During Christmas, for three days everybody ate and ate. To climax it all, his father threw coins in front of their mansion and the children, including some adults, fought for the shining silver.

Val had even taught Fay a song she could now sing. The tune was easy, but pronouncing all those jumbled words was difficult. She had fun stumbling through the phrases. He had to write it down for her:

> *O kaka O kaka, kabalat kapaya*
> *Sabian mu nang patas nung ena ca bisa,*
> *Keta man kekami dakal lang baluga,*
> *Mangayap la keka, biasa lang mamana.*

"All those K sounds," she complained. "What's this, a password to the Ku Klux Klan?"

"You should know," he said jokingly.

"And you call this a love song?" she asked, ignoring his remark.

"It is a love song," Val insisted.

When she asked him to translate it into English, Val hesitated. Not that he did not know the meaning; it was clear, but somehow, the words did not make sense, not the way they had to be said in English. Or perhaps they made sense, only he had already forgotten a lot of things about his country, like the meaning of this song. With a war on, the homeland seemed so far away it belonged to another world. No ordinary ship or plane could take one there. But first, there had to be peace.

"Well, it's got to have some meaning," Fay said while Val looked for extraordinary ships in his mind and peered at corners for the peace he could not find; there was no peace anywhere, "unless it's really not intended to have a meaning like 'Mares eat oats and does eat oats and little lambs eat ivy,' but even this nonsense has meaning. And you claim this one's a love song. Perhaps a G.I. tempting a native girl with his K-rations?"

"It's the girl singing," Val explained, ignoring the levity in her voice and words, and thinking of the shadows of hills around the peaceful valley he knew as a child; the little black men who came down to the plain to barter with the lowlanders, their funny way of talking, their appetite, their laziness, their devotion to their masters. "She's asking her beloved to tell her the truth, whether he still wants her because, she says, she will not mind the truth at all. Where she comes from in the nearby mountains, there are many other little black men, better than her lover, who were quicker with their arrows."

Fay was amazed at Val's explanations.

"Goodness gracious," she exclaimed, "is that what it means? I think the girl in the song is nuts. If my man doesn't want me any more, I'd know, he doesn't have to tell me."

"Well you're different," Val said, feeling that he had not quite succeeded in translating the true meaning of the song.

"Besides," Fay continued, "I don't think the girl was sincere. I think she just said that because it was the brave thing to do."

"Our women are a brave lot. They know how to take it. I imagine they have been taking quite a lot since the Japanese came."

Fay said, "If I believed you, your women have all the virtues. I bet, one day you're going to marry one of them, but of course. I have seen quite a few of them, doll-faced, pearly smiles, cute pretty numbers, fragile, handle with care . . ."

"None of them would have me, Fay. Besides . . ."

"Now you're being funny, Val. The few times you have taken me to some parties, don't think that I didn't notice the way the girls looked at you. I'm not that blind, sweetheart."

"No, of course, not. They just envied me, I guess, because you're always the prettiest in any crowd, Fay, believe me."

Fay was really an attractive girl. She dressed well and walked like a queen. Her complexion was radiant, especially in winter when the cold winds touched her cheeks. In a well-lighted room, it seemed her eyes gathered all the sparkle from the dazzling chandeliers and the lighted bulbs in America. But she had eyes only for Val.

The truth was, as much as possible, Val did not want his Filipino friends to see too much of Fay, although he felt good and proud standing beside her in a crowd with everybody looking at her. He was afraid some fresh guy might insult her or him in one of these dances and parties where the men drank heavily and the girls talked too much or his friends might come upon the two of them alone in his apartment. He lived in that constant fear, which he had not been able to hide from Fay.

When he was alone with her, in his apartment, he was always listening for doorbells. Even the ringing of the neighboring apartments' doorbells startled and annoyed him.

"What are you so fussy about?" Fay would ask. "If you don't want anybody to know we are here, then don't answer the bell."

"But it will keep ringing. Besides, it might be something important."

"Then answer it. I'll stay in here and won't bother you."

"I just don't want doorbells ringing. They drive me crazy," he said.

One day Fay told him, "Val, you are ashamed of me."

"Oh, no, Fay, I'm not," he protested, feeling deep in his heart that he was telling the truth because it was not really shame that he felt: it was something else, something he could not quite define. He wanted Fay around. Alone in the apartment, waiting for her to come, as she would sometimes promise, he imagined every footfall on the outside corridor was Fay's, and he would walk towards the door and wait until the footfalls sounded past, dying away in the distance, and a door would open and close somewhere, far away. He tried to read and smoked incessantly till his throat got sore and he would start drinking. He always had a bottle of gin in the apartment. He liked gin very much. Fay hated it. Once he forced her to take a sip and she clawed at her throat as she choked and tears came to her eyes. "It's like fire," she said, "it burns me, it turns my insides out."

Or he would turn on the radio, very low, so that he could hear the footsteps on the corridor outside, the clack, clack, clack of high heeled shoes that did not stop at his door. He felt the heels stamping on his breast, strange doors closing in on him like a vise, and he would drink some more, or put some clothes on and walk outside even in deep winter. He would just walk and walk, imagining every tall, slim girl was Fay coming towards him. When he got tired of walking, he would return to his apartment and imagine all sorts of things, that Fay was hiding somewhere to surprise him. Ever since he had given her a key to the apartment, he would sometimes hope that she would be around when he came. Once or twice this happened and he had been so delighted with her presence, he could not hide his happiness. She was sitting in the living room when he came in and he had rushed towards her, burying his head in her lap, letting her pass her fingers through his hair, fondling him like a child. "Thank God, you're here, Fay, I want you so," he had told her. But coming home to an empty apartment, he would mumble out her name, Fay, Fay, he would cry, picking up a tune that somehow fitted to the words, come, come, darling, I need you so, believing that wherever she was, she was going to hear him and come. There had been times in Fay's absence when he had to drink himself to sleep, but even then he would wake up before the dawn, hating himself, hating life, hating the world.

No, Val was not ashamed of her. If he only had his way, he would marry her and show her around to his friends with loving pride. But Val was weak, he was a coward, he knew he was a coward, he felt that he couldn't do anything, he dared not do anything without his father or mother, or the great family council, passing judgment on what he should do. Perhaps it was the way he had been brought up, but Val knew that he lacked strength. The fears that preyed on his mind had mostly to do with the great Rustia family, what they would think of a girl like Fay. Not that Fay was objectionable because she came from a broken-up family or that she herself had spent a few years in an orphanage, but they would object to his marrying anybody, just now, when they were out of touch. He remembered his father's words, "The greatest offense you could do would be to lose your head in America." And his own mother had expressed the same opinion.

One evening, the doorbell rang. Val jumped from the chair where he sat reading.

"Fay, someone's at the door," he said. "Shall I open it?"

"Go ahead," Fay answered as she combed her hair before the mirror in his bedroom, "I don't care. I'll soon be through and I'm going." At that time she still worked nights on Constitution Avenue.

Val opened the door. It was the old doctor, Val's professor in economics in the University of the Philippines and a dear friend of his father's.

"Oh, come in, Doctor," Val said, wondering how he was going to explain Fay's presence in his apartment. Or should he? Dr. L. P. Mendoza used to be a frequent visitor in the apartment and there had been times when he spent the night there. They would cook native dishes. He also enjoyed sipping gin fizz which Val could make very well. But that was before Fay came. His visits had not been too frequent since. The first time he came, Val was alone, but Fay was supposed to come, and he was so worried about it, he nearly told the doctor the truth, then. He wanted to. He wanted to find someone who would understand.

Val was happy to see the doctor. Yet he was afraid. He didn't know what to say or do about Fay's being there alone with him. Of course, he could take the old man to the living room or to the kitchen till Fay slipped out. But he would hear. Besides, Fay was not the sort who would slink away. She was honest about the whole affair; it was he who was the blithering coward. He had called himself many names.

"Chilly outside," the doctor said as soon as the door had closed behind him. Winter was straying early over the Potomac. The elms in the parks and in the circles had not yet completely shed their leaves; a little gold still remained on the promontories and hillocks.

Now, what was he going to tell him? Fay was coming out any minute. How was the doctor going to react to her presence? Would he act the way his father would, furious and merciless and completely lacking in understanding, thinking of nothing but family connection and money and the power that goes with it, the prestige of the hundred-year-old Rustia name?

Val remembered the days in New York when he practically supported the old man while he was sick and jobless. Then Dr. Mendoza would caution him about the girls whom he escorted around. He remembered his saying, "Be careful, Val, be very careful in this country. You're not just anybody." Spoken just like his father. "An indiscretion could be very costly. Not that you can't afford such things. I'm not thinking of that. I'm thinking of the greater price one has to pay at times, not necessarily in specie, but in something else. Then there's the matter of hearts. You just can't go around breaking hearts, Val. Your own couldn't be too immune, could it? Besides, everywhere, hearts are still on the gold standard, I suppose."

Now the doctor had removed his coat, shrugging his shoulders and stretching his arms as though to shake off the cold from the outside.

"The news seems good," he was saying, but Val was listening to the movements in his room, wondering what Fay was doing, what he himself was going to do.

Suddenly, he heard a door open, it was the bedroom door, and before he could think any further of what he was going to do next, there was Fay walking towards them in the living room.

The old man turned and bowed in greeting, showing no surprise at all. Fay was lovely, she was radiant.

"Dr. Mendoza, this is Fay. Fay Price. Fay, my good friend Dr. Mendoza," Val managed to say.

The old man acknowledged Fay's greetings and her smile with another courtly bow.

"Glad to have met you, doctor," said Fay after the briefest interval of silence, which extended, could have been awkward, but as it was, it seemed no interval at all except in Val's mind. "I was just going. Good evening."

"Good evening," said the doctor.

Fay threw Val a glance that said goodbye and strode out of the room, her head high, her manner of walking away, almost regal.

Val seemed to wake up from a trance and then quite impulsively he ran after her, catching up with her as she was about to open the door leading outside. He took her in his arms and kissed her rather passionately as he whispered, "Fay, darling, please try to understand."

Fay looked into his eyes and fondled his cheek with a gloved hand, saying, "You worry too much. Everything's all right. Now go back and talk to the doctor. You're such a boy. 'Bye now, sweetheart."

Val felt silly. She was so cool, so composed, why couldn't he be a little like her, frank, and good, and honest?

The old man was in the kitchen lighting the stove when Val returned.

"I guess, sir, I owe you an explanation," he said, feeling that now was the time to tell the old man about their affair.

"Maybe you don't," said Dr. Mendoza, putting the percolator over the fire. "I've known all about this, Val. You've not told me, but I know."

"You mean, everybody knows?" the coward in Val kept speaking up.

"Oh, no. I mean, your friends know you have a girl friend. They suspect you have several girl friends. This girl is one of them. That's what they say. But they don't know that she . . . well, your friends don't come here often, do they?"

"No, sir," Val answered, "not too often."

"The boys understand, I guess, but the girls don't. And they can be very mean about it. You know why. They feel that one of them should marry you, that is, you should marry one of them. Something like that. You know how superior they feel about themselves. At least, each feels superior enough to think she's worthy of you, every blessed one of them. They believe that you have no business getting into a mess with some American girl whom you're not going to marry anyhow."

"Why, the little fools!" Val cried with some heat. "How do they know what my intentions are?"

Soon after saying this he felt ashamed thinking that they could be right. Perhaps that was what made him speak too strongly. They knew what he himself kept refusing to admit.

"Well, you see, they are prejudiced," the doctor was explaining. "Prejudice is a funny thing. A brown girl is as much prejudiced against a white girl as a white girl is prejudiced against a brown girl. The whole thing really cuts quite deep, you know."

"Yes, I know," Val said, helping the doctor with the cups and the saucers rather mechanically, while his thoughts strayed deeper than what the doctor called prejudice. Prejudice wasn't involved in his case, prejudice was of the mind, and this was not a simple matter that could be thought out. This was a matter of feeling, a terrific mix-up that involved a pampered heir to millions, who was taking time to grow up, who perhaps would never grow up, a weakling, a blithering coward. There, he said it again.

"But how is it with you, boy? Tell me, who is the girl? Fay Price, is that her name? Are you going to marry her?" The doctor's voice sounded strangely familiar. Who spoke like that? Who called him boy?

"I really want to talk to you, sir," Val began.

"Go ahead, talk," the doctor said.

"Often, I've wanted to come running to you. I really need help, sir. I don't know what I feel towards Fay. Maybe it's just passion, maybe lust, I don't know; it could be love. I really don't understand myself, sir. There are times when I feel like running away from her, never to see her again, but there are times when I feel I cannot live without her. We say we love each other. We believe we do. But I don't know. I really don't know. When she's not with me here, I miss her. I feel like

shouting or going crazy. Maybe I'm crazy already. I see something she owns and I put it to my lips, a ribbon, an underthing, even a pin. Her fragrance, the smell of her flesh, is
in the room, she's everywhere in the apartment. I long for her
terribly. I know no peace till I see her. It's the same way with
her, she says, and she calls herself a fool, too, for feeling the
way she does for me. Sometimes, she says, stepping out of the
apartment, she vows never to come back, but she comes back,
she says she cannot live without me. I hope this doesn't sound
funny to you, sir, because it isn't funny at all. True, other
women have said the same things to me, practically the same
things, but there's a difference here, sir, but just what that difference is, I can't tell. I think I really love her, sir, only, I'm not
man enough to admit it. I'm afraid, but I don't know what I'm
afraid of . . . maybe, I know. Oh, doctor, please help me, help
us."

"I think I understand," said the doctor, "I understand too
well to offer any remedy."

"You mean there isn't any remedy?"

"I'm afraid not."

"You mean it will just blow over, sir?"

"I'm not even certain about that."

"Suppose I marry her?"

"That's your own problem, son."

Dr. Mendoza was unusually tight-lipped. As he had said, he
was not in a position to offer any remedy. Yet he was grateful
that Val had taken him into his confidence. After that evening, he was a frequent visitor to Val's apartment. The three
of them dined together, went to the movies together. Fay soon
became quite attached to the old man, and it appeared that
the doctor developed a fondness for her that surprised not
only Val but the doctor himself.

"She's a jewel, Val," Dr. Mendoza told him some months
later. "She's devoted to you. While she often admits that she
has no illusions, that she's too realistic to have any illusions, I
know it will break her heart if you leave her, Val. I don't think
she'll ever recover from it. She keeps asking about the Philippines, the people out there, your family, its position in the
country. She knows and it's part of the burden she bears from

day to day that she knows. You're in deep, boy. Remember what I told you. The trouble with hearts, they haven't gone off the gold standard yet. No, sir, not even in this country."

Dr. Mendoza was a great help, though, to the couple, in some ways. Val and Fay used to have many awkward moments of silence together when it seemed as though everything had been said, but there still remained a need for talk and nothing that they said meant sense. Sometimes they turned on the radio and the apartment filled with loud, strident songs, *Rum and Coca-Cola,* suggestive melodies, sentimental ditties, like *When the Lights Go On Again all over the World,* or the white cliffs of Dover with the valley blooming again . . . and then news, soon the war was going to end, there would be no more shooting, the doves of peace are in the air and the hunters have laid down their arms . . . Now, being a much travelled man and a very interesting talker, Dr. Mendoza often told the couple stories of many lands and all sorts of ways of life, to all of which Fay was the more interested listener. Her reactions impressed the doctor, not so much the intelligence of her comments and questions, but the feeling, the deep human feeling and understanding which she showed.

"Don't get fooled by that bold, uncaring exterior, Val," the doctor warned, "Fay's extremely sensitive."

"I know," Val answered.

"Why don't you marry her, Val?"

"Do you think I should, sir?"

"If you love her. You say you do. I think you do, only you're afraid. You're older than your years and yet you have not learned to face things . . . What do you know about her? Has she told you that she grew up in an orphanage, that she didn't have a decent childhood, that she has been practically alone all her life?"

"Yes, sir, I know."

"You're the best thing that has happened to her, or the worst. Don't think she doesn't know what sort of person you are. She's not dumb. She's a very good girl, noble, and honest. She's white through and through. I'm convinced that she loves you, Val. But whether you do, as you say, I'm not sure;

maybe, you yourself don't know. One of these days, you have to do something about it. This cannot go on and on, the way things are."

That day Dr. Mendoza left Val's apartment without saying good-bye. Val did not seem to notice it. For a long time he thought that truly, one day, very soon perhaps, there was going to be an end to what Dr. Mendoza called "the way things are."

In August, on Val's birthday, he was alone with Fay in his apartment, unaware that somewhere about the same time, a city in the East was burning and men were dying horrible deaths by the thousands. As a severe contrast, there was rejoicing in their part of the world. To the two lovers that mattered little, for in all the world that day, there were just the two of them. A little while back, she had given him her gift of love and none of her own fears. These she covered up with gentle thoughtfulness and a gaiety that hid the tears, or if they showed, could have been mistaken for tears of joy. She had even drunk to him, a toast in gin, his favorite. She had felt the fire burn her throat, and she clutched at it, laughing as she said, "It's wonderful. A little more of that would kill me, but I won't mind. Val, I love you, I love you." She wept on his shoulder, stifling the words she did not want him to hear, "Don't leave me, Val, don't ever leave me, darling."

They were preparing to go out to celebrate some more. Fay seemed composed, she didn't look too disturbed at all as she said, "Well, I guess this peace-around-the corner prospect calls for a double celebration, doesn't it, Val? It seems that soon, you'll have to go home."

Val turned quickly to look at her. She was standing before the dresser, looking at him in the mirror. There was Fay, real and alive, between him and the Fay in the mirror, no less real and looking just as sad no matter how sweet the smile on her face was and how casual her manner of asking, as though nothing depended on the answer.

But before Val could find the words to say, the doorbell rang, shrill and continuous, as though someone had leaned on it and would not budge until the door was opened.

Val stared at Fay, his heart pounding, his hands suddenly turned clammy.

"Well, don't stand there, answer the bell," Fay said with impatience, addressing his image in the mirror.

"I hear voices, many voices," Val muttered more to himself than to the girl who had not even turned to face him.

"Don't be a fool. Open the door," Fay shouted as though her anger, such as it was, could only be vented on the image of her lover.

Val turned to go, but came back to her and took her hands, drawing her to him as she faced him.

"I think I know who they are, Fay," he spoke low as though afraid to be heard, "I'll have to get rid of them . . . if I can. Meanwhile, please stay in here first . . . and . . . wait."

"Your . . . your Filipino friends?" she asked, sitting on the bed.

"Yes, I guess so, Fay," Val answered.

"And you don't want them to see me, is that it?" Fay asked in such a low voice, he could hardly hear her in the din of the ringing bell.

"Well . . ." Val could not think of what to say, "I mean, it's better you stay in here, huh, darling? It won't look good if they find you here with me, alone."

"Oh?" Fay had turned to the mirror and now bowed her head as though she could not stand what she saw, if there was anything to see, like the familiar suddenly becoming strange; but there was so much to hear; there was something wrong in what the voices said, about the continuous ringing of the doorbell.

"You just stay in here for a while, I'm coming back. I'll just talk to them and then I'll come back," one of the voices said. It was the nearest voice, the gentlest.

Fay did not turn nor look at him in the mirror as she heard the bedroom door close behind him. It seemed there were other bells, other sounds in the air.

Val had the main door hardly opened when they pushed in, barging in like a wave of invaders committed to take an island at a designated time. There were so many of them, one would think all the Filipinos in Washington had concentrated on this one door on this particular day. They were carrying bags of food and wrapped-up bottles of liquor, and they were singing, "Happy birthday to you . . ."

He recognized some of them, Sev, Joe, Mike, Eric, and Vincent, but the others just swept past him as though their objective was farther inland and there was no time to lose. The singing, broken up and off key, continued. The girls stayed behind and not till Val had smiled at one of them, did they stir. They stood there as though undecided whether to join the party or not. Some of them were leaning on the wall on the far end of the corridor, as though they were not with the party.

"Oh, Pitang, it's you, come, come in, all of you," Val was saying in a voice that surprised him, it was calm and sincere.

Pitang said, "Happy birthday, Val," and the others followed saying the same thing, the two Marias from Ann Arbor, Anita, Pilar, Helen, Angela; and the last, bringing up the rear, one of those leaning on the wall in the corridor, was Cielo, heiress to the Barranco millions, richer than the others, lovelier, and deeply in love, as everybody knew, with Val, and proud, prouder than gold. She didn't greet Val, just walked past him.

One of the girls said, "Kiss him, you said you were going to kiss him, now let's see you do it."

The girl referred to protested, "Look, I didn't say that. You were the one who promised to do it. Now, come on, I dare you."

Val stood by pretending to be interested, but all the while he kept listening to sounds, if any, from the bedroom. He knew, how well he knew, that whatever conversation went on in the living room, where they were now all gathered, could be heard in the bedroom.

"Safety in numbers," cried Helen. "Let's all kiss him at the same time!" The girls made ready to swoop down on him, but Val went among the boys, crying, "Help, help." The cry sounded meaningless. No, he could not act. How was he going to tell them, look, there's a girl in the other room, I love her, but what do you know about love, what will you think of her and me if you knew about us?

Some of the boys challenged the girls to direct their kisses to them. "You won't ever get to Val," he heard one boy say, "the fellow's getting a full diet."

They had spilled all over the hall and the kitchen, and talk and laughter went on simultaneously. Cielo sat in a corner, surrounded by the boys, listening to them and smiling, but she was watching Val. Every time he glanced towards her, she was looking at him.

Val didn't know what to do or how to compose himself. He could hear and understand only bits of what was said to him. He was thinking of Fay. How was she taking all this, would she remain where she was or would she come out and defy them all? Great God, she should not . . . and talk and smoke floated on about him while he managed to say something now and then and pretend how overwhelmed he was . . . happy birthday, Val, isn't it wonderful that your birthday should almost coincide with the dropping of the atom bomb . . . the Japs are cooked, we're going home . . . let's all get drunk, and that includes you girls, you should all get stinko . . . *bastus, bastus!* Oh where's the old doctor, Dr. Mendoza, where's he? Not around yet, but coming, you say? He should, after all, it was he . . .

Soon after, Dr. Mendoza appeared. Somebody had opened the door for him. Val had not even heard the doorbell. He didn't care for doorbells ringing now . . . Fay, Fay, I'm coming in soon, I'll explain, darling . . .

When their eyes met, the old man looked away, but fleetingly. He was smiling when he turned to Val again after acknowledging the greeting of those who had noticed his presence. He kept watching Val as though to say, now is the time, this is the moment, Val. There was pity in the old man's eyes as he watched Val trying to smile and get into the conversation in a voice that had no life in it.

Everybody was talking about the future, the Philippines, the letters that they had been receiving from home, the great, golden opportunities for making money out there, the things to do and bring. They were going to spend all the cash they could get hold of, even borrow, sell jewelry just so they could have enough cash to buy the things the country had so long been without, and net handsome profits, many, many times the original investment.

Take advantage of the situation, guys, the voices seemed united in that one refrain—*aprovechar*—and you, Val, ask your old man to send you all the cash he can, then buy all the cheap trinkets from Woolworth and you can sell them over there for real. They fall for such things, anything that glitters or shows the color of gold. We know one guy who has bought practically all the cheap watches in town, and shoes, summer wear particularly, boy, we can make a fortune on those things . . . Cielo, Cielo, dear, may I sign a promissory note, or you don't believe in notes, ha? . . . Write your old man, Val, he has money, surely you have heard from him?

Oh, yes, Val had heard from him. Father isn't too well, but he's going to live, but Fay, how are you going to fit into this madness, my lovely Fay, what are you doing now as I stand here like a petrified fool? You have been lonely all your life, Fay, you have worked for everything you own, you owe nobody. I have had everything all my life, Fay, everything, now I realize it, everything, but courage, give me courage, give me my own voice, not the echo of my father's, who will give me my own voice, who will give me courage?

The talk and the smoke and the noise swirled about him . . . Fay . . . wait a while, I'll be with you . . . Hey, Val, I bet your girl friend in the Philippines is just dying to see you now, have you heard, who's she, which family? what? oh, oh, Cielo . . . I had forgotten, *mea culpa, mea maxima culpa* . . . say, where's that lovely brunette we sometimes see you with . . . man, you sure know how to pick 'em. What are you going to do with her? No worry, man, you can always leave her to Vincent. That guy gets all the leftovers, he majors in handouts, garbage . . .

Vincent didn't hear this at once, but when he was told what had been said about him, he threw an empty can of beer at the talkative guy. The noise grew louder. Some of the girls were screaming and laughing hysterically.

Then Mike said, "You look sick, Val, you're pale, what have you been doing? Nobody told us you've been sick. And what are you doing, alone, on your birthday?"

One girl said, maybe it was Anita, "He was waiting for us, silly, he knew we were coming. Didn't you, Val . . . no?"

Val stood before them speechless as Dr. Mendoza tried to help by saying, "I was coming to fetch him, we have an appointment to eat out, but, I guess, there's no need for that now."

"I'm all right," said Val as Mike approached him to find out whether he had a temperature.

"He's okay," the doctor said, "He's just overwhelmed, aren't you, Val?"

"Yes," said Val, his voice truly an echo, "I'm just overwhelmed."

Now this could not go on and on. He must do something. Val walked away from the front room with some sort of just acquired stealth and a sudden cunning. Swiftly, he turned towards the bedroom. Then he looked back, hearing footsteps behind him. Dr. Mendoza caught up with him at about the same time the bedroom door opened and Fay came out, walking towards them. Val ran to her and seized her hands, crying "Fay, where are you going?"

What he saw amazed him. No doubt, she had been drinking. Her flushed face showed under the makeup, but it seemed she had touched her eyebrows anew and her eyelashes. Her eyes shone; there was a shimmer in their depths like tears. Her black hair, held back by a net, was a contrast to the smooth whiteness of her brow.

"Fay, darling," Val whispered, "what have you been doing?"

Fay shook herself free, ignoring his question, and went to the old man. "Hello," she smiled at him, "Please ask Val to let me join the party. I can't stand it any longer in the room."

Val and Dr. Mendoza looked at each other. Fay was dragging the doctor by the arm towards the sala. Yet he didn't move till he saw what he must have been waiting to see in Val's eyes. Meanwhile, some of those in the party, wandering by, had seen them and had hurried in to pass the word, so that when the three appeared at the door, there was no more surprise in the eyes that watched them.

"Good evening," Fay greeted the strangers, her voice clear

and firm, almost with some sort of authority, like the voice of an honored guest or the hostess herself.

There was no immediate answer, but finally the crowd found its voice with some fellows saying, "Welcome, welcome."

Fay started to say thank you, but Cielo cut in.

"Correction, please," she cried from her corner, her voice sharp, almost metallic, as she waved towards the boys, "Don't be improper, *caballeros. Que urbanidad!* We have no right to welcome the lady. Instead, we must ask, lady, are we welcome?"

It was not just what she said; her tone was a two-edged knife. Val wanted to put his hand on his breast where there was this sudden pain. He felt the blood drain from his face. He looked blankly in front of him. Where was Dr. Mendoza? Why didn't he say something?

"Look," Val began, wondering what he was going to say next. He had taken a step forward to call attention to something important he had in mind, but there he froze as though struck with stage-fright, having forgotten his lines. The faces before him shrivelled and shrank back, dissolving in mist. In the haze, he heard Fay's voice.

"Why, of course, darling, you are most welcome," she was saying, her tone too sweet, her accent cloying with dramatic over-emphasis, "But am I not too late to do the welcoming?"

Pitang had emerged from the mist of moving figures, huddled in corners. Now she was saying, "Doctor . . . Val . . . who will do the introductions? What happened to the men, suddenly demobilized? The war's still on, fellows, come on, introduce yourselves."

The doctor's voice came through edge-wise in the sudden talk and movement all over the sala. "Friends, this is Fay Price. Fay, these are Val's friends from the Philippines. They've come to give what they call an *asalto,* a surprise birthday party for Val."

"How nice," Fay answered, her accent still deliberately cloying and over-dramatic, "How sweet! I'm glad to meet all of you."

At the sound of the doctor's voice, the mist lifted, and now, Fay's . . . the figures in the room had assumed reality, the constriction in his breast didn't seem too painful any more, but still, Val searched his mind for what he wanted to say, something important, something everybody here should know. Val closed his eyes briefly.

Each of the boys gave his name as Fay looked towards each of them. The girls also introduced themselves, but Cielo simply looked at Fay, a half-formed smile in her lips, without giving her name. The old man was quick.

"Fay," he said, "this is Cielo."

Fay smiled, swinging a little towards the corner where Cielo stood. "How sweet you look," she beamed, standing a shade taller as they stood face to face like goddesses before a shepherd king, "how very sweet, just like your name."

"Oh, I didn't know you spoke Spanish," Cielo said, her teeth flashing as she smiled sardonically.

In Val's mind, the idea of a shepherd king vanished like a quick change of slides.

"Oh, no, I don't speak a word of it," Fay answered with a chuckle, adding as she whirled away to face another group, "but your name reminded me of the musical instrument."

There was a loud guffaw from one of the boys which started a chain reaction of other bursts of laughter and the hall was gay again. The doctor was smiling. Val sighed deeply as though all he needed to remember what he was trying hard to remember was laughter like this.

Fay was talking to the boys. They were all around her. Suddenly, she said, "Who's Vincent here? Come, Vincent, hold my hand."

Val swallowed hard. He looked around, seeking the doctor's eyes. Now he will never remember what he wanted to say. It was no longer important, whatever it was. There was only one thing to hope for, that the party come to an end. Meanwhile, no bruises, please, no wounds . . . not salt, but salve . . . no further wounds.

The boys were silent, drink in hand, but not too drunk, no doubt, to miss the implication of what Fay had just said. Vincent's head was bent. Now he looked up, searching the faces around him, his mouth working into a grimace. Someone beside him held his arm, pressing it gently.

"What? No Vincent? Who then will take care of me?" Fay asked, still in the dramatic pose and accent of the amateur, the novice trying hard, too hard.

Val rushed to her side and took her hands. They were deathly cold.

"Fay . . ." he began, but there were other voices shouting now, saying something happy; it was a song, "Happy birthday to you . . ."

Pitang approached Fay, shouting amidst the din, "Join us, join us!"

Fay joined in, her voice lost in the many voices, but just in time for her to sing the last chord, "Happy birthday, dearest Val, happy birthday to you," as she pressed Val's hand. Val wanted to kiss her right in front of them . . . by God, why not?

Someone tapped him on the back and shook his hand.

"Speak up, *hombre*, speak up," another fellow was saying.

"Speech, speech!" A chorus took up the cry.

Val smiled at them, shaking his head. "Thank you, thank you, everybody," he said.

Pitang walked to the center of the hall and raised her hand. As the noise subsided, she said aloud, "I'm happy to announce that the girls have prepared a few numbers for our entertainment and we challenge the boys to contribute 'counterparts.' "

Everybody applauded. There was some laugher, too, over the last word Pitang used, a common enough word in wartime Washington, and in this instance sounding so funny, yet apt.

The boys held an emergency conference. It was quick, decisive. Val smiled the ghost of a smile possible in a whirl of thoughts that came in and out of his mind as he sat on the rug at the foot of the chair where Fay sat. Mike accepted the challenge in the name of the boys. The girls booed him and he withdrew quickly for another conference of strategy with the boys.

"Oh, this is good," Fay smiled at Dr. Mendoza.

She was the only girl among the group of boys, but it was not too obvious because the three of them, Dr. Mendoza, Val, and Fay, sat a little forward, as though, indeed, they were the honored guests. All through the program, Fay sat with her elbows on the arm of the chair, leaning back comfortably, her fingers touching her temples. She changed position only when she clapped her hands or turned towards the doctor to say something or to listen to what he was saying. Once, she put down her hand and Val leaned close till her fingers touched his cheek. They were cold. Slowly, he moved his face till his lips touched her fingers. She withdrew her hand a little, but while everybody laughed and clapped, she moved her fingers close to his cheek again and fondled it with her finger tips. Val felt a current of fire go through his body sweetly, painfully. Will the party ever end?

The numbers were short and funny. One of the Marias sang *Ay Kalisud,* a plaintive love song from the Visayas. She looked toward Cielo as she sang as though the song were dedicated to her. As "counterpart," one of the boys sang "Pistol Packing Mamma" with slight variation in the lyrics to suit the contemporary Philippine scene as they read about it in the newspapers. Helen did an imitation of Carmen Miranda, swaying her hips while she sang, "Ya, ya, ya, ya, I love you very much . . ." It was terrific. Val turned to look up at Fay to see if she was enjoying herself. It was at this point she allowed her fingers to touch his cheeks in a caress.

The boys' contribution was even better. Sev did a solo imitation of an American boy dancing a boogie woogie with an imaginary partner, while he chewed gum as his face, all through the dance, assumed the stony look of one in a trance or in the grip of an ecstatic experience. He moved his feet to the rhythm of his jaws, he swayed and turned, pulling up his trousers, and losing his partner in the crowd of imaginary dancers. Without changing expression, he gyrated through the crowd looking for his partner, then finally he saw her, took her hand, and watched her go through the same motions, the expression in his face remaining the same, his jaws in perpetual motion. It was uproarious. Fay's laughter reached Val through the alien noise like a hail of welcome, as though it were the only voice, the only sound he could tell by heart.

During the buffet dinner that followed, Fay sat among the girls. She was telling them, "You're a happy people."

"We're trying hard," Pitang answered, "but as you can see, we're still exiles."

"And that isn't too easy, you know," one of the girls was saying.

"I know," Fay answered, "But that's over now, isn't it? Soon, you'll all be home."

"I don't think some of the boys are happy about going home," Cielo remarked as she jabbed at the little mound of food on her paper plate, "they are having such a grand time here."

Fay choked, spilling some of the food on her plate.

"Pardon me," she said, coughing softly into her hand.

Mike offered Fay an empty glass. He gave another to Cielo.

"Now," he said, "I'll pour each of you a drink, okay?"

A group had gathered around them. Val stood behind Fay's chair, searching the crowd for the doctor. He was right there, standing close to Mike, right beside where Cielo sat. As Mike was about to pour from a wine bottle into Fay's glass, she withdrew the glass and said, "If you'll excuse me, I'll be back." She walked away towards the door of the hall. In the sudden silence that followed, the clack, clacking of her shoes sounded like knuckle blows.

As soon as she was gone, everybody talked at the same time. All voices, a jumble of words. Val felt like leaving, too, and following her, but suppose . . . He had no idea what she was going to do. But she was not gone long. As soon as she appeared, the voices subsided, but Val heard someone telling Cielo, "Now, promise, be a sport."

Fay had returned with the bottle of gin in her hand. It was less than half full. God, no! Val thought.

"Here, let's drink from this," Fay suggested, giving the bottle to Mike, "I can't mix my drinks, that's the trouble."

Mike offered to pour, first into Fay's glass, but Fay demurred saying, "Cielo first, if you don't mind."

Cielo shrugged her shoulders and allowed Mike to pour.

"Enough," she said after a while.

Fay looked at the amount she had taken, then got as much.

"Now," said Mike, "let's have a toast. Everybody!"

Everybody stood up. At a signal from Mike, Dr. Mendoza moved slightly apart, holding up his glass.

"*Salud!*" he cried, "To your health, Val, from all of us."

Everybody drank. The two girls watched each other above the rim of their glasses. The others watched the two.

Fay finished her drink, but Cielo did not.

"It's like fire," she complained, coughing a little.

"That's what I said, too, the first time I tasted it," Fay said with a smile, "But you'll learn to like it. It won't take long."

"I don't think I ever will," Cielo replied, "I can't even drink champagne."

"Oh, that's different," Fay argued, "Gin's the real thing, it's the supreme test, that is, if Val's to be believed."

"Oh, then if Val said so, you must believe him, indeed, you must," Cielo said, her accent just as affected as Fay's, just as spurious.

"Indeed, I believe him," Fay answered, matching Cielo's accent, "I have learned a lot from him. He has taught me to drink, among other things. As you can see, the gin's almost gone. What you have drunk is practically our leftover."

Cielo's eyes flashed and, for a moment, they were on Val. Much to his surprise he found himself staring back. Everybody watched as though this were the second part of the program, in a different mood.

"Don't tell me," Cielo sneered, "you've just learned how to drink from Val."

"That's a fact, believe it or not," Fay smiled as though amused that she should sneer and disbelieve, "Tell her, Val."

"Yes, yes, I did, I taught her that, I taught her a lot of things," Val answered quickly. He did not grope for words. They were there. He felt bold and adequate, master of the situation suddenly. Even as he spoke, a surge of warmth pervaded his body and he wanted to move and gesticulate, he wanted to take on anybody. He continued, "Yes, I taught her that, but she hasn't learned. Right now . . . right now . . . but that's not what I want to say."

He went to Fay and took the plate from her hand. Then he gripped her arm and walked her to the window, near the radio, then turned her around, so that the two of them faced the crowd.

"Here," Val announced, his voice assured and firm. "This is what I have wanted to say all evening. Please listen. It's important." His voice faltered as his eyes fell on Dr. Mendoza. It didn't look like Dr. Mendoza. It was his father standing there, looking at him. With one hand still holding Fay by the arm, he gesticulated with the other, but the words didn't come too easily now. He looked again and it was no longer his father watching him, but Dr. Mendoza indeed. Val smiled as he saw encouragement in the doctor's eyes.

"I wish to make this announcement to all of you, my friends," Val began, the smile still broad on his face. "This lady, Fay Price, is my betrothed. She's the girl who will one day, very soon, be Mrs. Valentin Rustia."

In the wild applause that greeted his announcement, Val could not tell who was happy, truly happy about the news, and who was not. He did not care. He looked at Fay, who was smiling, while tears stood in her eyes. Even as he looked at her, Fay made a sudden motion of holding up her hands as though to call attention; she wanted to say something. After a while, there was silence again as everybody waited for what she, the chosen one, had to say.

"I thank you all," Fay began, her spurious accent, completely gone. "And I thank Val for so honoring me today. But as you can see, and as you will agree, I wish also to be heard. After all, I have not been asked, until today. No, no, I mean I haven't been asked yet. Therefore, I cannot give an answer."

There was murmuring over the hall.

"Fay," Val said, turning to her, "I ask you now in their presence, I beg you to, please, be my wife."

It seemed, Fay had not expected that. The answer she wanted to give choked in her throat on which she now pressed her fingers.

"Oh, Val," she cried, facing her lover, "Why did you have to do this now?" She spoke and looked as though for the moment she had forgotten the many eyes upon her.

"Answer, answer!" some fellows from the rear were shouting.

"Good heavens! *Que estupidos!*" it was Cielo's voice, exasperated, impatient, "What answer are you waiting for? Could there be another answer?"

"Oh, yes, there could be," Fay replied, looking straight into Cielo's eyes, then half-turned to Val and said, "Thank you for all the fine times, Val, thank you for this gesture, but, sorry, I'm not buying. Good night."

Before anybody realized what she was going to do, Fay had walked out of the hall. Val stood rooted on the spot, his eyes searching those upon him. Everybody talked at the same time. Their voices came to him like a suffocating wave and he felt like going under. Suddenly he felt a great need to cry, father, father! Just then, above the voices, rose one voice, shouting, "Go, follow her, you fool!"

At the sound of the voice he turned around and ran towards the bedroom. Just as he passed through the door, he heard the radio. Someone had turned it on. A voice was saying that there were rumors in the air, everywhere, that Japan had surrendered. An official statement from the White House was forthcoming. There were no other voices from the hall.

Fay was not in the bedroom. Her gloves and bag were not there. Val ran out fighting back a desire to scream. When he finally caught up with her, Fay was opening the door downstairs. He rushed to her and seized her hand. For a while they stood wedged between the swinging door.

"Darling," Val began, putting his arms around her, but Fay pushed him away and ran down the steps into the night. Val ran after her, but stopped under a lamplight and peered into the dark. It was the first time he had seen Fay disappearing in the darkness. Always, his memory of her was Fay, getting into the light, emerging out of the shadows, a radiance, a beautiful body aglow, against a dissolving darkness. This was different.

On his way back to his room, he saw the doctor standing near the door and for a while he thought it was his father waiting for him. In the hall, the party still waited for the final word from the White House about the surrender.

# FOOTNOTE TO A LAUNDRY LIST

*The August heat was too much even for those who were used to it.*
For Dr. N. B. Carlos, who had just arrived from the States, it
was unbearable. The damp, sticky heat made him sweat with
the least exertion, not necessarily physical, like thinking. He
had to change shirts between classes, which was quite incon-
venient as the only place in the University where he could
hide was the men's room, which smelled and had no lock that
would keep the door shut. It was worse before the rains. Like
now. The sun shone through overcast skies and faintly, he
could hear the rumble of thunder on the seaside. For this and
for another much stronger reason, he didn't look forward to
the hearing scheduled that morning which, he was afraid, was
going to be held again in the Chairman's stuffy office over-
looking the slums of the provincial city.

Somehow he felt relieved when a few minutes before the appointed hour, he received a note from the Secretary of the
Committee on Discipline, that the hearing would be held in
the President's air-conditioned office. The President, an old
man with young dreams, must be out of town again.

Dr. Carlos had been in the President's office once or twice
before and he remembered the soft lights, the softer voice of
the man behind the wide mahogany desk, the coolness of the
scented air. Getting into it, with the door closing automatically
behind him, was like stepping into a strange land with autumn colors and lights and autumn coolness; stepping out,
like walking into the hold of a freighter where the engines
are—and it always startled him to see outside the President's

168

office, fresh looking girls and cool boys, walking about the
burning campus as if it were the Elysian fields, instead of half-
naked men stoking furnaces, their hairy bodies dripping with
sweat.

When the heat became oppressive, he wished he had not
left the States. True, summer in New York was just as bad,
often worse, but there was always autumn to look forward to,
and winter and spring. And he didn't have to stay in New
York in summer. There were camps of all sorts up north just
below the Canadian border where there was work, cool
nights, and fun. There had been summers when he earned
enough to see him through school the entire year, penny
pinching, of course, all along the way. But he was used to that.

After getting his Ph.D., somehow the title felt like a load he
could not carry well whenever he was forced to take a menial
job, no matter how well it paid. Meanwhile, his cousins in the
Philippines had been writing him that now was the time to return and cash in on his Ph.D. and perhaps settle down.

At forty, he didn't feel too old; still, there were the bleak
years ahead he kept seeing before him. Dr. Carlos was not
unattractive, but he was shy. In class, his voice barely reached
the back row and his students had to strain their ears to understand this man with an accent who seemed to be saying
important things in a dull, ineffectual way. After a while, they
stopped trying to understand whatever it was he was saying.
He didn't make sense. His jokes were not funny at all, except
to him. He laughed loud and alone. If his students stayed
awake at all, it must have been due to something else like the
heat, or some of them must have kept hoping that with his
Ph.D. from Columbia and that accent, he was bound to say
something sensible one of these humid days.

His colleagues on the campus did not believe him at first
when he said that he had no family.

"You mean you don't have your family here with you,"
Professor Teves said.

"No, I don't mean that," Dr. Carlos explained. "I'm not
married, that's what I'm trying to tell you."

"You've been in the States these many years. How can you
still be single?"

"What's strange about that?" Dr. Carlos tried to defend himself.

"You are joking, Dr. Carlos. I understand that in the States . . ."

Here we go again, Dr. Carlos said to himself, closing his ears to the innuendo and the direct statement of free love in America, open love-making, immorality on the campus, right in girls' dorms and homes, with membership in fraternities and sororities mere excuses for promiscuity. He had heard these stories himself and had seen men and women in summer camps where he had worked, cuddling under blankets. But it was not as general as it was made to appear. As far as he was concerned, he remembered only the hard times, the struggling to keep himself in school, the little hurts and the big fears. He closed his mind to these, shaking his head.

At forty, he easily chickened out. Never endowed in his younger years with the courage one often needed to go through an experience without bruises, at forty, he had practically given up trying to do anything about, say, getting himself a wife, which, to him, required courage, more than anything else.

As an adolescent before and during the war, he had liked girls in the neighborhood in Palomar where he lived with an elderly brother who had a family of his own. He used to beat class in night school to accompany a pretty seamstress who had just arrived from Pampanga and didn't speak Tagalog well. He gave her lessons, which they both enjoyed. He liked her eyes and her dimples and the frightened way she clutched at him the first time he kissed her on the mouth at the foot of the bamboo stairs, where chickens roosted and cackled all over the place while the lovers struggled in the dark. Pacing loved him with a trembly, panicky sort of love while she kept insisting that he didn't love her as much as she did, which he persistently denied until later when he realized that she was, indeed, right, he didn't. He couldn't remember now how their little affair had ended. How did they break up? Did they? Pacing was a cry-baby. She still looked pretty when she smiled with her tears rolling down her cheeks and her body shaking in his arms as though it were a fearsome thing to be there in his arms where she loved to be. Where could she be now? He had heard that she was married now to someone from her own province who sold floor wax and looked like Jose Rizal. Perhaps he had loved her after all. The trouble was, he never knew. How did one know?

Paula Weeks still wrote to him. She worked with the United Nations in New York. If she loved him, why were her letters without passion? Most of them read like reports to the Unesco. Paula and he had classes together in Columbia for a term, then she quit school—work at the office was too much—and later transferred to NYU, where he would have gone, too, except that he would have to lose residence in Columbia where he had started working for his Ph.D. Yet he knew she did—love him. She told him so. In the middle of a statistical peroration on the rising cost of commodities, she wrote: "I had to hand-carry an urgent note to the Librarian of the Public Library and suddenly, I realized that I had been there before—with you. How I missed you, darling. I love you, Nap. When are we ever going to see each other again?" Her question sounded more like his own.

Perhaps if he had decided to stay on in the States, he could have married her, but he had no intention of taking her to the Philippines. Paula wouldn't be able to survive any day in August. She would go nuts. At least, she would keep saying, "I'm going nuts" till she might actually be and to show her sympathy, he might go loco himself. Now, of course, if he were rich enough, say, to install her in an air-conditioned home, that would be different. Paula loved winter. He used to meet her after classes when he was not too busy with his research and they would walk arm in arm through the snow and the slush. Paula loved every moment of it.

All memories of tenderness with Paula were winter memories. She was closest to him in winter despite the heavy suits they wore. In summer she couldn't bear for him to touch her. When they held hands, their palms stuck wetly. It was embarrassing.

He had met her family once, soon after his graduation, when she took time off from her work at the United Nations and together they visited her family in Oneonta. Paula introduced him as Dr. Napoleon Carlos. It was the first time he heard himself called doctor and he was not too happy about it. Paula's father sold canned food of different kinds, but not once did Dr. Carlos get a chance to sample one of the flavors right in their own home.

There were freckles on Paula's nose and under her eyes. They started to show in spring. By summer, they were in full bloom. In winter, they were mere smudges that he tried to wipe off, asking, as he fingered each one of them, how long will you have these freckles? Why do you ask, you don't like them? I love them, he had replied, kissing her nose lightly. I'm going to have them all my life, she told him.

Yes, he could have stayed on and married Paula. She would be twenty-one now, no, twenty-two, much younger than he, but she wouldn't believe him when he told her his age.

It was raining hard when the *Doña Nati* left the wharf in New York harbor and Paula stood in the rain waving to him as he sought her out in the mist and waved back as soon as he recognized her. The rain was cool on his burning lips. They had kissed and kissed till his lips were sore and he felt a dryness in his throat neither rain nor drink could quench. During those days, while he was preparing to leave, Paula was around most of the time, helping him. There was the problem of what he was going to do with his winter suits. I'll store them for you, Paula said, until you call for them, adding, will you call for them? You know I will, he said. When? Sooner than you think, he told her with conviction. Shall I make out a receipt, she asked. He pulled her to him and they kissed again. How about that for a receipt, he said. No, I must list these suits, she said. She took them out one by one and folded them neatly and drew out a list in her own hand. Scribbling something like a footnote at the bottom of the list, she called his attention to what she had written: not responsible in case of fire or damage or loss for reasons beyond our control. They laughed over the words, familiar to those who bother to read what is written in small print on laundry lists, but many times afterwards, he could not recall what had made them laugh together.

Paula was brave. Yet, on the last day, on their way to the

pier, she broke down. Perhaps I won't ever see you again, she cried. Give me a rain check, he said, trying to laugh over what he considered great wit, considering the rain and all. She smiled, too, laughed a little, but all he remembered was her whispering, I love you, I love you, as she clung to him in the rain.

It was a lonesome, miserable trip back home. He was sick every day of the first week, but at every port, he mailed her a letter. Each letter was a passionate avowal of love, no mention of seasickness. And he meant every word he wrote her then and since. Paula was quick to answer in the beginning. She owed him a couple of letters now.

Dr. Carlos read the notice signed by the Chairman of the Committee on Discipline: ". . . therefore, it is important that you attend this meeting to hear the side of the girl accused by Mrs. Estrella L. Vivo of having illicit relations with her husband. The accused, Miss Magdalena Barin, is a sophomore in the College of Education."

Miss Barin sat in the middle of a half-circle of chairs, everyone occupied by deans and senior members of the faculty, old men in varying stages of decay, and one woman, the bespectacled Dean of the College of Education, who spoke with a sidewise tilt of her head as if every word she said rang out banners and cheers for the victory of virtue over vice. Veins stood out on her hands and forehead like submerged eels trying to come out and join the fun. Dr. Carlos felt young in their midst and wondered, as he often did, how he happened to be a member of this particular committee in the University.

Miss Barin was small and perhaps still in her teens. She wore no makeup although her hair was neatly brushed back. She kept changing her position as though no matter how she sat, she was still exposed, naked to this half circle of old eyes observing her every move, listening to every nuance of her speech, as if tone could hide a lie and change of pitch repress the truth.

The Committee Chairman was direct and abrupt. Like a veteran orchestra leader, he had the members of his Committee under his baton, and they responded as he expected them to, in harmony, following up lead questions, stressing exclamations of censure, as though everything had been rehearsed and the long hours of rehearsal were now paying off magnificently. So wrapped up was everybody in the hearing, no one paid attention to Dr. Carlos who followed every movement of the girl, asking no questions himself, as though his part in the orchestra came near the end of the piece. Meanwhile, therefore, he could rest his cymbals or his flute on the music stand.

Are you acquainted with Mr. and Mrs. Sulpicio Vivo?

Yes, sir.

When was the last time you saw Mrs. Vivo?

Mrs. Vivo?

Yes, Mrs. Vivo.

Or perhaps you want to tell us the last time you saw Mr. Vivo.

Anything you wish, sir.

All right. When was the last time you saw Mr. Vivo?

Just a few minutes ago, sir.

Just a few minutes ago?

Yes, ma'am. He met me at the gate of the University and he told me he was leaving for Manila.

Did he say why he was leaving for Manila?

He was going to, I think, but I told him I was in a hurry. I had an appointment with . . . with this Committee at 9 o'clock.

Do you know why he was going to Manila?

As I said, sir . . .

What do you think?

I don't know, sir.

Did he ask you to go with him?

Ma'am?

You heard me.

Yes, ma'am, I heard you. But why should . . .

Could it be that he had quarreled with his wife—over you?

I don't know, sir. He didn't have a chance to say . . .

When was the last time you saw Mrs. Vivo?

The other Sunday, sir. At a party in their house. It was a birthday party, their youngest child's, I think.

Who invited you to the party?

Mrs. Vivo herself.

Oh, you are friends?

No, ma'am. We just know each other.

How did you get to know each other?

Her husband introduced us.

When was this?

At a dance. On the campus, sir. Last February. Valentine's Day.

The charges are: that you have been seeing each other, you and her husband; that you have been having illicit relations. What do you say to these?

We have been seeing . . . I mean, he has been seeing me. I have asked him to go away and not see me every time he comes, but he insists, saying he can't help himself. But we have never had any of what you call that kind of relations.

Mrs. Vivo has a statement here supposed to have been made by a policeman who had been detailed to keep an eye on you and Mr. Vivo.

That's all lies, sir! He was a bad man, that policeman, threatening me, forcing me to sign all these lies. I told him he could kill me, but I wouldn't sign. Why . . .?

Where does Mr. Vivo see you?

At home, I mean, at the boarding house where I occupy a room with other girls.

You are not alone in your room?

When I'm alone, yes, sir.

I mean, you don't occupy a room all by yourself?

No, sir. I can't afford that.

One allegation here is that Mr. Vivo buys you things.

He has bought me things, but I returned them, at least, those I could return.

What do you mean, those that you could return?

When he brings food from the Chinese restaurant, the other girls immediately begin eating it up, how can I return that *pancit*? Besides, he looks so hurt when I insist that he take back what he is giving me, sometimes I don't have the heart . . .

Oh, come now, what girl doesn't welcome gifts?

Ma'am?

Mrs. Vivo went to your room once and found their radio on your bed. Do you deny this?

No, sir. But I have a radio, of my own. It's out of order. Mr. Vivo himself volunteered to have it repaired. Meanwhile, he lent me his radio.

Does he go to your room when the other girls are there?

Yes, sir. He just shows up.

Have you ever been alone together?

Yes, ma'am.

Where? In your boarding house? Somewhere else?

In my boarding house. Once . . . we went on a picnic, but it rained that day.

So?

We went back to town early and had lunch in a Chinese restaurant. All by ourselves.

Do your parents know about Mr. Vivo?

I have no more parents, sir.

Who supports you?

I have an aunt, sir. An old maid aunt who's a teacher.

Why do you go out with a married man?

I'm sorry, sir.

Do you love him?

I don't know, sir. He's very kind to me.

But you know he is married.

Yes, sir. But I'm not marrying him. We don't . . .

Does he make love to you?

No, ma'am. He simply likes being with me, he says. He laughs a lot when we are together.

Mrs. Vivo claims that she found some of her husband's shirts in your room.

Yes, he leaves his shirts there.

Scandalous!

Ma'am? I thought nothing about it. You see, one day he complained of the heat. It was too much, he said, I think I should bring an extra shirt so that I can change when I have to. He catches cold easily. So the next time he came, he brought a shirt with him.

These shirts Mrs. Vivo found in your room were clean.

I washed them. They were dirty.

Scandalous! You're not his wife.

When my father was still living . . .

Never mind your father.

I'm sorry, ma'am. I didn't think it was wrong. He has been so kind. It was not hard to do. I wash my own things.

Why did you enroll in my College?

I want to be a teacher, ma'am.

What kind of teacher do you expect to be?

Well . . . if I could be like my aunt . . .

Does your aunt know about Mr. Vivo?

I have not seen her since June. She's always busy, sir. She teaches in a coastal town far from our barrio. She has to take a boat. When the weather is bad . . .

According to this police report . . .

That's all lies, sir, I told you.

Let me read it to you.

I have already read it, sir. It's lies, lies!

For the sake of the members of the Committee as a matter of record . . .

I move that it be off the record, if that is your wish, Mr. Chairman. We all have been furnished a copy. Besides, what are we trying to do?

Don't you know, Dr. Carlos?

I'm asking you, Mr. Chairman.

Let me quote from the Code of Conduct, Article VII, Section 1, sub-section 3: "In extreme cases, such as gross immorality, the student may be expelled from the University. Expulsion debars any student from admission in any public school or private school recognized by the government." Have I answered your question, *Doctor*?

Thank you, sir, but don't you think you have asked Miss Barin enough questions?

You haven't asked a single question yet, Dr. Carlos.

No, I haven't. That's right. I thought everybody was doing pretty well.

Dr. Carlos tried to smile as he looked around him. The lady Dean's face was a mask of fury.

The girl had turned towards Dr. Carlos. "All I ask, sir," she said, "is that I be allowed to quit . . . if you don't want me here anymore."

"It isn't as simple as that, I'm afraid," the Chairman interrupted her, "unless the Committee . ."

"She's asking to be allowed to quit," Dr. Carlos said with more volume than accent in his voice and tone. "That's good enough for me. As a matter of fact, if you are asking me, sir, she doesn't have to quit."

"What?" the lady Dean practically screamed.

Dr. Carlos turned his back to her, saying, "I find the accused innocent of all the charges. She told us everything, a lot of things she didn't have to admit, she has admitted to us. She is innocent, I repeat."

A sob broke out from the center of the agitated circle. The crumpled handkerchief she covered her face with was too small, the tears fell on her lap, through her fingers. As her body shook, her short legs dangled and her moccasins fell on the floor under her chair where she had kicked them. A stained bit of paper shaped to fit the inside of one shoe stuck out like a tongue.

Finally, the girl raised her head, her face wet and her eyes red and swollen. Her lips trembled as she talked.

"Sir, may I quit?" She looked around, then felt for her shoes under the chair without taking her eyes off the powerful people.

No one spoke.

"Go home, child," Dr. Carlos said, softly, but his words rang in the room like the strangest sound, not flute, but cymbals crashing out of tune.

The girl stood up, seeking the door. Standing so close, Dr. Carlos noticed how short and frail she looked. Where was she going now? To fry out there on the burning campus? Where else? There was no coolness anywhere. It was not going to rain for a long, long time. My, how short she was. If Paula put her arms around her, she would have to stoop and Paula wasn't very tall herself.